THE IMMORTAL SOUL

THE JOURNEY TO ENLIGHTENMENT

Case Studies of Hypnotically Regressed Subjects and their Afterlives

DAVID RIPPY

ISBN-13: 978-0-692-15064-1

This book is dedicated to the inquisitive, the ascended masters who have come forth to share their wisdom through the ages, the traveler who diligently searches for the keys to the meaning of life and all its mysteries, and most of all, to the children who someday will grow up and carry forward the secrets of life and teach others what they have found.

Table of Content

Preface

~

"Know thyself and thou shalt know all the mysteries of the Gods and the Universe"

— Inscription on the Ancient Greek Temple of Apollo at Delphi

Enlightenment: It's the Promised Land within described by spiritual and philosophical leaders like Jesus, Buddha, Confucius, and Plato, among others who have brought forth the mysteries of life and given us glimpses of our immortal self. It's a state where one comprehends the inner-workings of life itself and understands that the soul is immortal and that what we know as "real life" is but an illusion.

I won't claim this book will unlock all the mysteries of these ascended masters' teachings from different times on all nations of earth. However, every reader will come away with a greater understanding of the possibilities of the infinite. For some, it may be a whisper in their subconscious and for others a deepened pool of knowledge and comprehension of what lies beyond our mortal, physical state.

Use these pages to travel with me to the shores of the New World through the eyes of a British First Mate in the Royal Navy who finds himself in grave danger. Venture to the World War II battlefields as a Nazi military officer in a tank battalion. Follow along with me into the subconscious and super-conscious states of eight subjects placed there using hypnotic induction where they can tell us vivid and startling details of their past lives. Those interviewed will learn about the entangled nature of their past and present lives, such as the woman who discovered she'd been in the same ill-fated romantic pairing as when she was a settler on the U.S. prairie.

These case studies have been directly transcribed from the session recordings. For anonymity purposes and confidentiality, the subjects' names are not used. The names, places, years, and pertinent details surrounding the lives they share while in deep hypnosis, are at times illuminating, emotional, difficult and challenging. Conversely, the lives they describe after death are hopeful, enlightening, peaceful and joyful in the majority of cases.

Beyond the initial hypnotic induction to place the subject in a subconscious or super-conscious state, I have no idea what will unfold during the session. Like me, the reader will be spellbound, mesmerized by the way the subjects' past and present lives interweave and by the profound wisdom shared on the other side.

Every case study is unique, each subject recounting a different version of heaven, or hell in one case, when the participant leaves that life. Some recall meeting Jesus, Archangels, Angels, departed loved ones, spirit guides, and their individual Council of Elders at the end of that life. Afterward, when reviewing that life on the other side with their council, some are given succinct advice and discussion on how well they did with their life lessons chosen before incarnation with their spirit guides. In some cases, their councils offer direction on what they need to work on to move forward in their current life.

One deeply regressed subject offers, quite unexpectedly, information on the current "Age of Aquarius" — the cycle humankind has recently entered — and shares deep insights for humans. A few others share their soul-color evolution, an indication of their soul evolvement as pioneered by Dr. Michael Newton. Subjects also revealed the colors of the souls they encountered on the other side.

The journey to enlightenment is never easy, and there are no shortcuts. As Confucius said, "The true path to the higher realms of enlightenment is the slow path." It's only through good effort in studying the "enlightened ones," going inward, and standing on the shoulders of those who came before us and shared their wisdom that we can light our way. Going inward — through chanting, meditation, hypnosis, quiet self-reflection, or utilizing other methods — is the path to not only the inner-worlds of possibilities but also the awareness of the interconnectivity of everything.

The past lives and life-between-life regressions of these eight subjects is a tool to aid in self-discovery. Each subject learned more of their immortal and divine nature in the process and discovered more about themselves on a deeper level. Enlightenment is an individual journey, a journey that has no end. As you walk along your path of self-discovery, over time and with effort, you will be amazed how far you have come.

Introduction

~

"Do not believe in anything simply because you have heard it. Do not believe in anything simply because it is spoken of and rumored by many. Do not believe in anything simply because it is found written in your religious books. Do not believe in anything merely on the authority of your teachers and elders. Do not believe in traditions because they have been handed down for many generations. But after observation and analysis, when you find that anything agrees with reason and is conducive to the good and benefit of one and all, then accept it and live up to it."

— Buddha

Hypnosis has fascinated me since my youth when I first saw it performed on a Boy Scouting trip with a troop of about thirty other scouts. One night of the outing, all of us crammed into one of the larger tents and watched in awe as an elder scout hypnotized a volunteer. We listened spellbound to the hypnotist as he began using basic relaxation techniques to put our friend into what appeared to be a hypnotic trance.

Understandably, the majority of us were initially skeptical about what seemed to be a carnival sideshow display of mesmerism. The demonstration appeared to have the fingerprints of two scout pranksters all over it. We continued to watch suspiciously as the hypnotist commanded his volunteer to straighten his arm so that nothing could bend it. We all took turns trying. I noticed that as every scout struggled against his rigidly locked arm, he remained calm, and it didn't appear he had to exert a lot of energy during this trial.

It was easy to notice that the hypnotized participant's countenance and facial expressions were mild, almost robotic, as every scout strained to bend his rigidly locked arm. None of us succeeded. It was as if he were partially removed from the event, but not entirely. Next, the hypnotist instructed his subconscious participant that he had incredible pain tolerance, was impervious to fire and burns, and was invulnerable to the prick of a needle. Everyone in the tent straightened up, suddenly more attentive to the spectacle, knowing that for an average, awake person that would be impossible.

But on this night, hypnotized by the elder scout, he was capable of things none of us, volunteer included, had ever witnessed. He didn't seem to feel pain. He had an uncharacteristic physical strength. He was bolstering his body with reinforcement from somewhere in the innermost recesses of his mind.

The tent grew strangely quiet. We watched as our hypnotized friend didn't flinch, jerk, or yell out in anguish as the hypnotist stuck a needle into his arm several times and ran a flame along its underside. All convinced, we asked for the demonstration to end, wanting to spare our friend any further testing. I felt like I had just witnessed something magical.

Eventually, the hypnotist instructed our friend to awaken feeling indomitable and robust. He was quiet at first, just blinking his eyes. After a spell, he shared his experience, explaining that he felt enveloped by a sense of calm at first, followed by an ever-strengthening feeling of relaxation and control. He "just knew" that his arm couldn't be bent, and he never felt the pain of the needles or fire. He was able to go along with the suggestions from a semi-detached place of power and inner self-control. He confirmed that upon waking up, he felt better and more energetic, just as he was instructed.

I sat there eagerly absorbing what I'd just seen and heard. It was at that moment that I began to appreciate the powers of the human mind. It was the dawning of the realization that positive, self-reinforcing dialogue was beneficial and could induce a profoundly relaxed state where incredible things were possible.

A decade later, flipping through local television stations, I stumbled upon a talk show featuring a hypnotist doing a demonstration of past-life regression. I thought back to the hypnotized scout in the tent and the unusual powers he demonstrated while in a deeply regressed hypnotic state. Already believing in reincarnation, I stopped channel surfing and started watching.

Over the next hour, she captivated me with her remarkable skills, using past life regression techniques on three audience volunteers. The first, a middle-aged businessman, began recounting life as a Chinese teen in the early 1600s. He detailed his clothes, shoes worn during the era, where he lived, as well many more facets of his life. The second, a man in his mid-thirties, detailed his time as a woman who'd just opened a new dress shop that catered to flappers and other people with "pizzazz" in New York City in the roaring twenties. The third, another man, described his life as a starving woman in India, begging desperately for rupees so she could eat. Each could provide remarkable details, from one subject describing hamlets in China to another navigating the side streets of Manhattan. Remarkably, that man had never visited the Big Apple in his current life. That was all I needed to see — I had to try it.

I wanted to experience a hypnotic state to see if I had led other lives and learn more about myself in the process. In my further research, I discovered that reincarnation had been in the bible. One hundred and sixty-five church elders during the Second Council of Constantinople in 553 A.D. had reincarnation removed from the text after being leaned on strongly by the emperor at the time.

Before that, rebirth was an unquestioned pillar of belief taught by the early church fathers, such as Origen, St. Gregory, and Basilides as a matter of course. It was written in the bible, after all. These teachers, as well as their congregants, understood it logically: "How could a loving, benevolent God give one person a wonderful, happy life, and another soul a sad and challenging experience if a soul was only to have one life?" Early church leaders understood this, and reincarnation remained a pillar of Christianity for over 500 years after Christ's death.

A diabolical plot was launched in the court of the Byzantine emperor, Justinian, to have reincarnation removed from the bible. In the generation before 553 A.D., reincarnation was an uncontested fact. This fundamental dogma was even reinforced by the Council of Chalcedon in 451 A.D. Who could believe that the ascension of one man to head up the Eastern Roman Empire in 527 A.D. would have such an impact on the truth? Let alone the lives of so many?

The purpose of this book is not to question whether or not that text should have been removed. There still remains quite a mystery if the topic of reincarnation even came up in some of these Council meetings. For every article or historian that you read, there are countervailing opinions on both sides whether reincarnation came up or it didn't. I personally think that reincarnation should never have been removed from the bible, as it changed the course of Christian theology and the understanding of reality for so many. Here are some modern-day statistics: Fifty-one percent of the world believes in God. Fifty-one percent of people believe in reincarnation, twenty-six percent "aren't sure," and twenty-three percent think that "we cease to exist" at death.

I'm confident of a higher power. I felt reincarnation had merit, but I wasn't sure at first. Like many in the U.S., I was the product of a branch of Christianity, and in my youth attended a Presbyterian church with my parents. I had never heard anything in church about reincarnation growing up. I realized later, as I approached adulthood, if I just took the words of what the minister was saying to heart without researching, I was doing myself a great disservice. I would be no better than a simple follower with no original or well-reasoned opinions of my own.

I decided to begin a self-exploration and looked up the number of the hypnotist I had watched on television and made an appointment. To someone on the street, unaware of her hypnotherapy background, she appeared as a kind, gentle grandmother in her early seventies. She looked well-versed in baking tasty chocolate chip cookies, as opposed to someone who could help a client explore their subconscious and bring forth the hazy memories of an earlier life.

After driving to her house, situated in a well-kept middle-class neighborhood, her husband greeted me at the door and welcomed me into their den. She came in with a smile and after small talk about why I wanted to explore a past life we started the session. After a brief hypnotic induction, I began to find myself in a mild trance. During her starting questions, I wasn't confident in my mind whether the information I was receiving felt accurate or was even real. Initially, her questions didn't elicit many answers. I just never felt sure. She guided me more deeply into the recesses of my subconscious with stronger in-depth induction techniques. I found myself slipping into a deepened hypnotic state, and as if from a distance, her voice instructed me to picture a dwelling or structure that I might have once known. After a while, a picture of the inside of a dark cabin surfaced in my mind. I was surrounded by handmade furniture, crude cooking utensils — some homemade by their appearance — with a big cast-iron pot hanging over the fireplace. She asked me to open the door and go outside. Pushing the wooden plank door open and stepping outside, the sun nearly blinded me.

Once my eyes adjusted, I saw only green fields extending to the horizon and dotted with the occasional tree before spotting a woman in the yard. The hypnotist asked if the woman I saw was me. "No," I answered immediately, "I think that is my wife." After looking at her for a while, I knew her name was Elizabeth. I watched her, noticing her wearing a simple blue and white checked dress with a small matching cap on her head. She appeared to be making butter in an old churn. I stood there just observing, having been instructed that she couldn't see me. I noticed a young girl, roughly eight-years-old, run quickly past my wife. I knew immediately she was my daughter. Her red hair was styled in two pigtails that sailed behind her as she whipped around the front yard playing. I knew her name was Amy Catherine. Eventually, I remembered my name in that life: John Adam Miles.

It was like watching an old, colorized family home movie. As I viewed the scene in my mind, the memories of that earlier life became clearer. As we went forward, the amnesia blocks that had kept the knowledge of that life locked deeply away in my subconscious fell away. Despite looking and acting remarkably different than I do in this life, I knew it was me.

The longer I watched, the more familiar everything seemed, and I began to realize things about myself. I'd become orphaned when I was about eight and was left abandoned in New York City. By the 1850s, I was in my mid-thirties and toiling over some pretty good soil, judging by the health of the crops. I was working as a farmer living roughly thirty miles southwest of Lexington, Kentucky. My frame was tall and slender, capped with dark, long hair. My nature was to be distrustful of most people, and I was not much of a talker. In my current life, I'm outgoing, and so I was surprised to find myself with such a reticent personality.

At first, the images had a hazy and unfocused feel to them, but as the session went on, the images, thoughts, and feelings began to grow clearer in my mind. I was bewildered; was that me?

I visited the hypnotist twice more, each session spaced about six months apart, wanting to see if the same life would appear. During the next regression, I was the same man and was able to see other snapshots throughout that life. The hypnotist nudged me to recount a memorable time that I was proud of but that someone else might not find as remarkable. I "saw" myself winning a long-rifle shooting competition; my prize was a nice-sized turkey. I viewed myself wearing a long black coat and top hat standing with ten other men dressed similarly. All of us were drinking a pint of homemade beer served from a wooden barrel on the back of an old horse-drawn wagon.

After those first two past life regressions, I assumed the life I'd see during the third session would be the same and that it was the most recent life before this one. Expecting more of the same life, I set up a third appointment. The hypnotist induced me into a deep hypnotic trance and asked me once again to picture a dwelling and describe it when I was ready. She added on a reminder that I was there to observe and not get emotionally involved.

As the gray faded from the scene, it was as if a veil was pulled back off my blocked memories, revealing a window into a different life than I'd expected. These were different memories than I had experienced before, all the different lives I'd led stored somewhere in the dark, locked-up annexes of my subconscious. I described to the hypnotist what I saw. I saw myself on a lawn about twenty yards away from the right side of a beautiful white house edged by a wrap-around porch. It was situated to face the beautiful blue waves of an immaculately kept beach, just fifty yards away. The sun winked in the sky, partially hidden at times by passing clouds, and the temperature was warm, a perfect beach day.

I immersed myself in the reverie until her voice, as if from a great distance, cut into my scene and asked, "Do you see yourself?"

"No," I said. She followed with, "Why is that? It sounds like a perfect day." Suddenly, I understood why the house was empty. Viewing inside the house from a distance, as if my eyesight had taken on that of an eagle, I noticed linens covering all the furniture, the ghostly reminder of a family who wasn't there. In a somber tone, I shared, "I think I died."

After a pause, she gently reminded me that we were only to observe and would not get emotionally involved before telling me to go five years earlier in that life. I now saw myself laughing in an expansive kitchen surrounded by people close to me, feeling they were my family and a few very close friends. I stood in the back of this crowded kitchen, and when I glanced at my former self, I was taken back. I saw a tall, attractive brunette. That revelation rocked me as it wasn't what I expected. I was pretty sure I would see my previous life as a man again.

We were all laughing in this kitchen together eating breakfast. I saw everyone passing around a paper which appeared to feature Babe Ruth on the cover. We were laughing over another scandal that "the Babe" had found himself embroiled in. It had the feel of the early 1930's as I recounted the scene, but I felt conflicted since the present me didn't know anything about Babe Ruth beyond that he had played for the Yankees at some point. Before the regression, I hadn't known about his illustrious personal life, the records he had set, or much beyond the fact that he had played baseball. Somehow, during this session, I found myself knowing more about Ruth than I knew in this life and could recall details of his life that I'd locked away in mind.

As the reel of my past life flickered on, I saw pictures of a successful woman, a writer for an East Coast art magazine, who was married but had no children and lived in Connecticut. I summered at this beach property, witnessing myself at different times standing on the spacious front porch and looking out over the ocean. This beautiful beachfront property on Cape Cod belonged to my father. As the session went on, I remembered that he was a prominent Boston doctor, well known for his work with heart patients.

Later, I learned what had happened to me. Sometime in my mid-thirties, I developed a form of cancer that was untreatable and died. In that life, I knew of Edgar Cayce's work and believed in reincarnation. I aspired to write a Pulitzer Prize-winning novel, but I never did. I was at peace with that in my last days, and a belief in the after-life and reincarnation made my passing easier.

After that session, I recognized the immortality of the human soul. Still early in my exploration, I did not yet have the groundwork laid or the wisdom I would need to pursue a greater understanding of the afterlife and the journey of the soul. Nonetheless, my three past-life readings had piqued my interest, and I needed to know more.

Over the following years, I continued my journeys inward, read many good sources along the way, researched deeply, and learned of others with similar interest in the hypnotherapy field. I read many published psychologists' accounts of patients who had near death experiences, used hypnosis in past life regression therapy, and those who had pioneered the regression work of life between lives.

I eagerly followed the work of Edgar Cayce, the ascended masters, Dr. Michael Newton, Dr. Byron Weiss, and the University of Virginia Department of Paranormal Studies, among other sources that dated back through the ages.

In time, I came to what I consider an irrefutable conclusion: The soul is immortal and reincarnates in different and varied lifetimes to foster soul growth and evolution. Eventually, those souls that have had enough experiences and lessons and had many, many lives, no longer have the need to reincarnate. Their consciousness becomes part of the collective "over-mind" or "God." These souls assume other tasks in God's creations as well and become what we know as ascended masters, wise ones, and benevolent teachers who help other souls with their advancement and evolution.

There is no fast track to enlightenment. One who feels they've discovered the state concludes eventually that it only exists in the collective consciousness or the general repository of all knowledge, lives, actions, and thoughts. Through research, meditation, and hypnosis one can shed their earthly veil and awaken from a cosmic amnesia state to discover their true nature as divine, unique, and immortal beings. This repository of all knowledge is known by many names, as the Akasha, the Bible's "Book of Life," and the Egyptian "Book of the Dead." This storehouse is one where each of our souls contribute every life, experience, thought, deed, and action on our every journey, all added to the collective consciousness.

Knowing that, we can grasp that "Enlightenment" is never static, is always changing, and grows and evolves with each life undertaken. Everything flows back to the collective consciousness, Source, Spirit, Yahweh, Brahma, or whatever name you use for GOD in your culture.

The limitations of the mind are only one of degree. The more significant your exploration of knowledge, wisdom, and enlightenment, the greater your mind will expand and your consciousness with it. One who seeks will find, one who searches will be rewarded, and one who takes the journey will bring him or herself closer to the truth.

My expeditions inward using meditation, mantras, chanting, and hypnosis, along with vigorous study have helped me on my journey in pursuit of what happens to us at death and why we incarnate. It also endowed me with a greater understanding of the worlds and dimensions beyond earth's plane.

Perhaps you think it was a random event that put humanity here, something from our Darwinian past that brought us to current day. Or maybe you believe that something of a Divine nature carefully created what we know to be life. To others, perhaps you feel it was a combination of both. Either way, join me as we pull back the curtain for these eight subjects uncovering their past lives, what happened at their death, where they went, and the souls and councils they encountered on their journey.

It is my sincerest hope that this book will open your eyes a little wider, broaden your knowledge, and deepen your grasp of reality. For those open-minded but skeptical, or unsure like I was initially, hopefully the pages of this book will give you new insights on age-old questions, such as "What happens after I die?" "Why am I here?" "Will I see my departed loved ones again?"

The Man with the Burned Face

~

This reading was conducted for a female client in her mid-twenties. It was her first past life regression and first time being hypnotized. Much of the hypnotic induction was left out and begins at the end stages of the process to bring about a very deep, relaxed state. Though it was the first time the subject had been hypnotized, her practice of meditation helped to put her in a deep, somnambulistic state fairly quickly.

DAVID: You're floating along, so relaxed. Counting down from five to four. Down to three and sinking deeper and deeper. Feeling this bubble just take you in and carry you where it wants to. As I count down to two. Floating above a beautiful sea of flowers, as I count down to one. And as you continue to float along, you start to feel images come into your mind of another time, another life. As you are floating along, just let everything happen to you that you see. You can start to visualize something, perhaps a location or a house. You see yourself somewhere as you're floating along in your mind. You begin to see, perhaps someone that doesn't look like you, but you just know it is as you're floating along in your mind's eye. Tell me what you see.

SUBJECT: [Snoring softly]

DAVID: You're not sleeping, but deeply relaxed, hearing my voice. So, think about it for a minute, what do you see or what do you hear or smell?

SUBJECT: [Long pause, deep breathing] Burning wood.

DAVID: You see what again?

SUBJECT: Smells like burning wood.

DAVID: Does it smell like a fireplace or...

SUBJECT: It does outside… it's burning outside.

DAVID: It's burning outside. Okay. Is it a controlled fire? Or does it smell like it is in the distance?

SUBJECT: It's far away, but not that far.

DAVID: Are there woods around you?

SUBJECT: No.

DAVID: But you can smell it. Do you see where you are?

SUBJECT: Living on a street.

DAVID: You are on a street and you smell burning wood. Are there houses on the street? What does it look like?

SUBJECT: [Long pause] I see a man.

DAVID: Okay...

SUBJECT: I opened a door. A man with a burned face was standing there.

DAVID: Was he burned by the fire?

SUBJECT: I think the building caught on fire. [Pause] I don't think he got out.

DAVID: But he somehow made it to your door.

SUBJECT: Yeah.

DAVID: Are you in your house or somewhere else?

SUBJECT: I'm in the house now.

DAVID: Was he coming to your door, maybe for help?

SUBJECT: I think so.

DAVID: Were his clothes burnt too?

SUBJECT: Yeah, they were covered in soot.

DAVID: Does he look like he's in a lot of pain?

SUBJECT: No, I think he's… a ghost.

DAVID: So, he doesn't appear to have a solid body?

SUBJECT: No, he does but he doesn't look real.

DAVID: Is he talking to you with words or is he talking to you with his mind?

SUBJECT: He's not talking. I opened the door and he was there, but he wasn't there a minute ago.

DAVID: Okay... [Pause] and what are you wearing? What do you think you are wearing?

[Asking a subject for a clothing description early on brings their focus toward themselves and lessens the impact of witnessing unfamiliar sights like ghosts. Often, apparel or dwelling descriptions can help to determine possible timeframes for the life they are viewing.]

SUBJECT: [Pause] I can't see myself.

DAVID: Okay... but you can see your house?

SUBJECT: I'm just in a hallway at the front door.

DAVID: Now is the man still standing there on your porch?

SUBJECT: Yeah.

DAVID: Did he tell you what he wants?

SUBJECT: Yes, he said, "This is my room."

DAVID: So, you think he might have lived there before you?

SUBJECT: I think so. I think it's a boarding house.

DAVID: Do any names of locations come to mind?

SUBJECT: I don't know. I don't know.

DAVID: Do you know your name?

SUBJECT: [Pause, deep breathing] Liza.

DAVID: Liza.

SUBJECT: Yeah.

DAVID: That's a pretty name, what does it look like inside, when you look around, does it look old inside or what time period do you think it is?

SUBJECT: It's old. It's… 19... 1900s. 19- I can't tell. 1916? 1917?

DAVID: Now do you think he was burned when he lived there? Or was it somewhere else? Do you think there was a fire, or do you think maybe it could have been a war?

SUBJECT: He's not in a uniform, and I think it was a fire in the house. I think he fell asleep with his pipe burning. I think that's how it happened, that's how he burned his face.

DAVID: So, you think this is the boarding house where he burned himself. Where is this house located? See what he says.

SUBJECT: He says Cambridge.

DAVID: Okay... and does he have a name of the house or street?

SUBJECT: [Hesitates] I think it's Cads… C-A-D… Cadbury… Cadbury Street.

DAVID: Now is it Cambridge in Boston?

SUBJECT: Yes, Massachusetts

DAVID: So, Cadbury St. and you feel it's around 1916?

SUBJECT: Yeah.

DAVID: You know your name is Liza.

SUBJECT: Yes.

DAVID: Do you know your last name?

SUBJECT: [Pause]. It starts with 'TH.'

DAVID: Does it have two syllables?

SUBJECT: Thornsten? Thurston?

DAVID: Just let it come. See if you see it in your mind.

SUBJECT: Thompson. Thompson.

DAVID: And you feel it was on Cadbury St?

SUBJECT: Yes, Cadbury Street.

DAVID: So, Cadbury sounds right. Now, since you were there, and the ghost man was there, do you have a number for the house on that street? What number pops in your mind for that street address?

SUBJECT: [Pause] I can't see a number.

DAVID: That's fine. If you walk outside... can you walk outside for me?

SUBJECT: It's cold.

DAVID: It's cold out? So, it is around wintertime you think?

SUBJECT: No, it's not, but it's cold.

DAVID: So, it's cold out and is the wind blowing a little bit?

SUBJECT: It's windy.

DAVID: I don't want you to go too far outside, but do you remember if the number of the house is on the front of the house or is it way out on the street?

SUBJECT: Thirty-three. Number thirty-three.

DAVID: So, you feel pretty good that it is thirty-three, right?

SUBJECT: I saw the number on the house.

DAVID: Good and how long have you been there you think?

SUBJECT: Not long.

DAVID: Less than a year?

SUBJECT: That's right.

DAVID: And were you renting a room?

SUBJECT: Yes.

DAVID: How old do you think you were then?

SUBJECT: [Pause] Um, I think I'm older… in my thirties or forties.

DAVID: And how did you happen to come to live there? Did you come from somewhere else or what?

SUBJECT: Yeah. I think I work… in someone else's house.

DAVID: Good. And what do you do in the other person's house?

SUBJECT: [Pause] I'm a nanny.

DAVID: Little children, I guess?

SUBJECT: Yeah.

DAVID: How many are you watching?

SUBJECT: Three.

DAVID: Three children. Do you know their names or ages?

SUBJECT: The oldest is eight and the youngest is still a baby.

DAVID: Do you know their last name, the family that you work for?

SUBJECT: Stanley.

DAVID: Stanley. Do you know the mister of the house's first name?

SUBJECT: Robert.

DAVID: What's the wife's name that you work for?

SUBJECT: [Pause, deep breath] Eleanor.

DAVID: So, Robert and Eleanor Stanley. You think that's pretty accurate?

SUBJECT: That's it.

DAVID: Now, what does Robert do in the Cambridge area?

SUBJECT: He… works in the steel plant. He... he owns it.

DAVID: So, he's pretty well off I guess.

SUBJECT: Yeah.

DAVID: Is it a big house?

SUBJECT: Yeah, it's big.

DAVID: So, it's a nice house.

SUBJECT: Mhm, yes, it is very nicely decorated.

DAVID: Now the steel company that Robert works for, can you see the name of it?

SUBJECT: It starts with a 'B', but I can't see the rest.

DAVID: Do you think it is two syllables?

SUBJECT: I think it's two.

DAVID: So, he owns the steel company, but he didn't name it after himself, I guess?

SUBJECT: He, I think, inherited it from someone else.

DAVID: Does it employ a lot of people?

SUBJECT: Yeah.

DAVID: So, it is a pretty well-known steel company.

SUBJECT: Yeah.

DAVID: What do they make with that steel? Do they do a lot of different things? Do you know?

SUBJECT: I don't know.

DAVID: But you think it starts with a 'B', can you see the next letter in the word?

SUBJECT: 'U.'

DAVID: So, it is a 'B-U' what's after that?

SUBJECT: 'C.' I can't see the rest.

DAVID: So, it's "BUC' and how long have you worked for this family? What was their last name again?

[As you will notice in other readings in the book, I find that checking a subject's recall of pertinent and specific details later in the session is a good idea. Asking the same questions provides three things: a sense that they are living that life, they are deep enough to absorb the life fully, and they are not fabricating the information they're giving.]

SUBJECT: Stanley.

DAVID: How long have you worked there?

SUBJECT: Less than a year.

DAVID: So, you took a job and then moved, I forget, what was the name of the street you moved to?

SUBJECT: Cadbury Street.

DAVID: So, you moved there to take this job, is that correct?

SUBJECT: Yeah, a friend of mine told me about it.

DAVID: So, you got a good job with a prominent family in the Boston area.

SUBJECT: That's right.

DAVID: And you think you are in your thirties maybe?

SUBJECT: Yeah, my thirties or forties.

DAVID: What color is your hair now?

SUBJECT: It's dark; it's brown of some shade.

DAVID: And your name is Liza, is that, right?

SUBJECT: Yeah, Liza.

DAVID: Do you have a middle name?

SUBJECT: I think it was Marie.

DAVID: So, you are pretty sure Liza Marie, what was your last name again?

SUBJECT: Thompson.

DAVID: Liza Marie Thompson. And have you been… did you come from another nanny job in Boston, or did you come from out of state, or out of city?

SUBJECT: I don't remember.

DAVID: Okay. Is this one of your best jobs you've had in that life?

SUBJECT: I like those kids.

DAVID: They were fun?

SUBJECT: They were smart. They were well behaved.

DAVID: Do you remember the name of the eight-year-old?

SUBJECT: Prudence.

DAVID: So, they had a daughter named Prudence. Did she have a middle name?

SUBJECT: I don't know what her middle name is.

DAVID: But her last name was Stanley correct?

SUBJECT: Yeah.

DAVID: Now when you look at that beautiful house, let's say you're standing outside now, like you are about to go to work one day, what street is your job located on?

SUBJECT: [Pause] Starts with an 'S'. It's the name of a tree. I think it was Sycamore. I think it was Sycamore.

DAVID: Are you sure it was a tree?

SUBJECT: Yeah, a tree, the name of a tree.

DAVID: Now when you look at their front door or front of their house, what was the house number? Do you remember?

SUBJECT: 118.

DAVID: 118, and when you think about it now, and let it sink in, Sycamore seems like the name of that street. Is that, right?

SUBJECT: I think so.

DAVID: Or it could have been Cedar and begin with a 'C'?

SUBJECT: No, I think it was an S. Sycamore sounds right.

DAVID: And how far from work was the boarding house where you lived?

SUBJECT: A trolley ride away.

DAVID: So, it was a trolley ride away, a mile maybe, half a mile?

SUBJECT: Not that far.

DAVID: So, it wasn't that far of a ride on the trolley. Do you remember what they charged for a trolley ride to the house?

SUBJECT: Just two coins.

DAVID: What were those coins denominated as?

SUBJECT: Uh, a five-cent and a penny I think.

DAVID: So maybe like a nickel and a penny, or six cents?

SUBJECT: Something like that… seven cents or six cents.

DAVID: So pretty reasonable or does that seem like a lot of money back then?

SUBJECT: I made a good amount of money working for that family.

DAVID: So, you were doing pretty well at that age, weren't you?

SUBJECT: Well, I didn't have kids either, so I only had my own expenses to worry about.

DAVID: Do you remember that house on Cadbury? What do they charge you for boarding? Do you remember? Was it by the month?

SUBJECT: Yeah, it was a monthly amount.

DAVID: Do you remember how much that was?

SUBJECT: I think it… [Pause]… I think it was seven something. I think seventy dollars—something a month.

DAVID: So, was it pretty nice boarding house for roughly seventy bucks a month?

SUBJECT: It was big, yeah.

DAVID: So, did you have a nice room?

SUBJECT: Yeah, it was nice. But that man was always there… that ghost.

DAVID: Did you see him regularly?

SUBJECT: Yeah.

DAVID: Now, did you have the ability to see ghosts back then or not?

SUBJECT: I could see him.

DAVID: Was he a nice ghost or what?

SUBJECT: I think he was lonely.

DAVID: Okay... and you were able to see him. Did other people ever see him, or you don't know?

SUBJECT: No, they didn't see him, but sometimes they'd hear him.

DAVID: How big was this boarding house? How many rooms did they rent out?

SUBJECT: It was four-stories tall.

DAVID: Wow, so it was a nice size.

SUBJECT: Yes.

DAVID: Do you remember what the outside looked like?

SUBJECT: It was brick.

DAVID: When you look at that man, what was his name? Did he ever tell you?

SUBJECT: I don't remember his name.

DAVID: He died in a fire, but no one knew his name.

SUBJECT: He didn't tell me his name; I never knew it.

DAVID: But he let you know he was in a fire in the house smoking a pipe, is that right?

SUBJECT: I think so.

DAVID: Now how long did you work for the Stanleys? Do you remember?

SUBJECT: Yeah, for six years.

DAVID: Then what happened? Did the kids go to school?

SUBJECT: No, the money… something with the money. The stock market or the stocks that he had… his business went bad. He poorly invested, I think — something foolish in his business plan. Like I said, I think he inherited that steel business and other stuff, I don't think he knew what to do with that company.

DAVID: So, he didn't do well in the steel business.

SUBJECT: Yeah, I always got the impression that his wife was the one with the real brains and not so much him.

DAVID: So, after a while, they couldn't afford to pay you, is that correct?

SUBJECT: Yeah, I think they had to move.

DAVID: So, you think they had to sell their nice house because they couldn't afford to live there anymore?

SUBJECT: I think so, yeah.

DAVID: Do you remember what they paid you, by the week or maybe by the day or the month?

SUBJECT: No, by the week.

DAVID: Do you remember how much you were paid by the week, starting out? Or when you left?

SUBJECT: Hmm… I think it was close to thirty-two dollars a week when I first started.

DAVID: Then it went up to what? Fifty? Fifty-five dollars?

SUBJECT: Yeah.

DAVID: So, you got paid pretty well back then, is that correct?

SUBJECT: Yeah, I did get paid well. I also knew languages. I spoke French and I spoke… Danish? I think it was Danish. So, I could charge more because of that.

DAVID: Were you teaching the kids languages?

SUBJECT: Yeah, I taught the girl French.

DAVID: Was that the older daughter?

SUBJECT: Yeah.

DAVID: And what was her name again?

SUBJECT: Pru. Prudence.

DAVID: And she was pretty fond of you as a teacher, wasn't she?

SUBJECT: She was a really bright little girl.

DAVID: Did she learn violin or any other things while you were there?

SUBJECT: She played piano.

DAVID: So, she was a bright, talented, nice young girl.

SUBJECT: Yeah.

DAVID: Well, so when you left, she was what, right around fourteen roughly?

SUBJECT: Yes.

DAVID: And was she sorry to see you go, since I guess you had become friends with her?

SUBJECT: She was sad.

DAVID: And how was Mr. Stanley handling this? Did he seem very edgy? How was he when his business started failing?

SUBJECT: I think he was cheating on his wife.

DAVID: So, you think he was cheating on his wife. Now I want you to go forward in that life, you were what, around thirty-five, forty-something when you left?

SUBJECT: I think I was forty-five.

DAVID: I want you to go forward to when you were fifty-five. Do you see yourself now?

SUBJECT: [Long pause] Yeah.

DAVID: And where are you working at that time? Do you remember?

SUBJECT: I work in a store for… women's clothes, a dressmaking shop.

DAVID: Are you still in your boarding house?

SUBJECT: No.

DAVID: And where did you move to?

SUBJECT: I moved in with my friend.

DAVID: Was it less expensive?

SUBJECT: She was not married, and neither was I.

DAVID: Do you see where your apartment was or where you lived?

SUBJECT: We had a cottage.

DAVID: Did you have pets?

SUBJECT: No, but there was a cat that used to come around… sometimes she would feed it.

DAVID: When you look at that cottage, can you describe what it was made out of?

SUBJECT: It was made out of stone.

DAVID: Out of stone? Do you remember what street that cottage was on?

SUBJECT: No. It wasn't really on a street. It was on a property with a very large house, basically another estate. We lived in the cottage there.

DAVID: Was this another rich family or something?

SUBJECT: Yeah, she worked in their kitchen.

DAVID: Your friend did?

SUBJECT: Yeah.

DAVID: And where did you work?

SUBJECT: In the dressmaker shop.

DAVID: That's right, and do you remember the name of that shop?

SUBJECT: [Pause] MNK.

DAVID: MNK?

SUBJECT: Yeah.

DAVID: Was it owned by a husband and his wife?

SUBJECT: By a woman.

DAVID: And where in Boston was it located? Was it downtown?

SUBJECT: I don't remember. I wasn't familiar with the city.

DAVID: But you were able to take trollies and get around, right?

SUBJECT: Yeah.

DAVID: How long did you work at that dress shop?

SUBJECT: For about twelve years.

DAVID: So, you worked there for a pretty long time.

SUBJECT: Yeah.

DAVID: I want you to go to the end of that time. Take your time. And describe how you're looking now in that life.

SUBJECT: Well, I'm very ill.

DAVID: Sorry to hear that. Do you know what you are ill from? What did the doctor's say?

SUBJECT: They said mumps, but I think it was a fever. Rheumatic fever.

DAVID: That's what it felt like, and you kind of knew that later, is that right?

SUBJECT: I knew I was seeing things, and my temperature wasn't normal. I was very sick.

DAVID: Do you remember what the doctors gave you to try and make you feel better? What were the medicines?

SUBJECT: [Pause] I think I was given penicillin…but I was allergic to it.

DAVID: Did that hurt you?

SUBJECT: It gave me hives. And my tongue swelled.

DAVID: And if it was penicillin, how old were you then?

SUBJECT: I was in my sixties.

DAVID: Do you see what hospital you were in? Were you in a hospital or just at home?

SUBJECT: I was at home.

DAVID: And did you get well again or not?

SUBJECT: No, I don't think so.

DAVID: So, I want you to just relax and visualize in your mind while you were feeling sick and we are just observing that life. Do you see yourself when you passed away? How long were you sick for?

SUBJECT: Less than six months.

DAVID: It just didn't get better, it got worse?

SUBJECT: Mhmm…yes.

DAVID: Do you remember how old you were when you passed away?

SUBJECT: [Pause, deep breath] Hmm. I think I was 63.

DAVID: Does that number sound real to you?

SUBJECT: Yeah, 62 or 63. I think I didn't make it to my birthday.

DAVID: And when was your birthday, do you remember?

SUBJECT: In the spring, in May. I died in April.

DAVID: You almost made it, didn't you? What day was your birthday? Do you remember what day in May?

SUBJECT: It was… [Deep inhale] May 14th.

DAVID: May 14th. And do you remember what day you died in April?

SUBJECT: I died on the 26th.

DAVID: So, you were pretty close to the birthday, weren't you? A couple of weeks away.

SUBJECT: Yeah.

DAVID: Were you trying to stay alive long enough for your birthday or were you in too much pain?

SUBJECT: I think I didn't even know what day it was.

DAVID: You were that out of it?

SUBJECT: Yeah. I kept seeing the man with the burned face.

DAVID: Did he come to you while you were dying?

SUBJECT: Yeah, I saw him. He sat in the room with me.

DAVID: Did he comfort you?

SUBJECT: Yeah, but he didn't sit next to me, or anything. He just sat there in a chair across the room. I guess he just wanted me to know that I was not by myself.

DAVID: Now, while he's sitting in the room, where's your roommate during all of this?

SUBJECT: Well, she had to work.

DAVID: So, you would be at home sometimes by yourself except for this ghost in the chair, is that right?

SUBJECT: Well, yeah.

DAVID: So, he kept you company until she came home.

SUBJECT: Yeah, and sometimes he stayed after she was home.

DAVID: But your roommate never saw him, is that correct? Was she sensitive to seeing ghosts or did you tell her about it?

SUBJECT: She saw something, but I don't think she knew what to believe.

DAVID: She thought maybe you were hallucinating?

SUBJECT: She thought I was hallucinating. She thought my fever had spiked, but she saw his shape once.

DAVID: So, she let you know she saw his shape.

SUBJECT: She said she saw something very queer.

DAVID: Let's think about this history, you're all nice and relaxed, and you're seeing the room you are in. What did the room look like?

SUBJECT: There is a window, a big window to my right-hand side, and the bed was in the middle of one wall.

DAVID: Did you have any pictures on the wall? Do you remember?

SUBJECT: A picture of my parents from when they were first married. And they were…

DAVID: What were their names?

SUBJECT: [Sigh] Their names… Clifford and Mary.

DAVID: And their last name again was?

SUBJECT: Their last name was Thompson.

DAVID: Clifford and Mary. Did they live in that area of Boston most of their lives?

SUBJECT: I think they lived outside the city.

DAVID: Do you remember when you were younger what your father did for a living?

SUBJECT: He was a postman.

DAVID: Oh nice. And how many brothers and sisters did you have? Do you remember?

SUBJECT: I was an only child. My mother had health problems. She couldn't have other children.

DAVID: Now did your mother work?

SUBJECT: No, she didn't work.

DAVID: Did your father deliver mail all over that area?

SUBJECT: Yeah.

DAVID: Was he with them a long time?

SUBJECT: Yeah, he worked up until the day he had a heart attack.

DAVID: Sorry to hear that. How many years was he with the postal service do you think up until the heart attack?

SUBJECT: I want to say about forty years.

DAVID: Was he with the United States Post Office?

SUBJECT: He worked for the government before he worked for the post office. But he worked for the post office for thirteen, fourteen of those years.

DAVID: He took a different job with the government. What did he do for the government before the post office?

SUBJECT: I think it had to do with taxes.

DAVID: He was a pretty smart guy?

SUBJECT: He was smart, yeah.

DAVID: Well they sound like very nice parents. Did you like your parents?

SUBJECT: I did.

DAVID: Good, because they sound like nice people to me. Let's go back and look at Liza while she's there. Sounds like you had a wonderful childhood, I presume. Do you remember where you were born?

SUBJECT: Maynard? Mayweather?

DAVID: Is that outside Boston in Massachusetts?

SUBJECT: Yeah, two hours from the coast, I think.

DAVID: Did you go down to see the ocean once in a while?

SUBJECT: Yeah, I remember it as a child.

DAVID: Did you take trips there?

SUBJECT: Not often, but yes.

DAVID: How far again was this from the ocean? Did you ever know?

SUBJECT: I don't know, maybe two hours?

DAVID: So, you were a little bit inland, where you went to the beach.

SUBJECT: Yeah.

DAVID: So, you were born in Mayweather or Maynard. Do you remember what shore they liked to go to? What city was that near? What was that called?

SUBJECT: I don't remember. I was too young.

DAVID: So, as your mother's health got worse, your trips to the beach decreased I presume.

SUBJECT: Yeah, I took care of her.

DAVID: So, you the daughter were taking care of your mother in her sickness, is that right?

SUBJECT: Yeah.

DAVID: That's a good daughter. Do you remember what issue she had with her health? Do you remember? What affected her the most with her health?

SUBJECT: [Pause] Her lungs were bad. I think it was asthma.

DAVID: Asthma, okay. Now you told me, give me your birthdate again, please.

SUBJECT: My birthday was May 14th.

DAVID: And what year was that?

SUBJECT: Hmm. I don't remember. [Pause] Eighteen-something.

DAVID: So, it was eighteen-something.

SUBJECT: 1870-something I think.

DAVID: Look in your mind and what were the last two digits of 1800?

SUBJECT: 1876.

DAVID: So, you were born in 1876, and you think you lived in either Mayweather or Maynard. Something with a "May" in it.

SUBJECT: Yeah.

DAVID: Your name was Liza...

SUBJECT: Marie Thompson.

DAVID: Okay. You think it was May 18th, 1876, you were born, is that correct?

SUBJECT: May 14th.

DAVID: Sorry, May 14th. Well I want you to think about all of this for a moment. And I want to go back to your last moments. Can we do that?

SUBJECT: Yeah.

DAVID: Do you see when you passed away, you told me it was in April... 23rd?

SUBJECT: 26th.

[As you noticed, the subject didn't waver on the date of her birthday or date of her death. She was deeply in the life as Liza Marie Thompson and though I tried to trip her up, she remained steadfast with her responses.]

DAVID: So, April 26th. And what year was that?

SUBJECT: 1940.

DAVID: So, you are pretty sure it was around 1940?

SUBJECT: Yes.

DAVID: Let's do this, I want you to sit there and remember those last moments of your life. All we are doing is observing, very relaxed. Describe to me right when you passed away, what happened?

SUBJECT: I saw a light. I thought it was coming from the window, but then it wasn't really coming from any one place, it was everywhere. And I remember seeing the man with the burned face, and he was standing over me, and I asked him where we were going. He didn't say anything at first but then he said, "You'll see when we get there." I don't remember anything after that.

DAVID: So, you see the light, and it is around you, and the elderly man with the burned face was there.

SUBJECT: He wasn't that old. He would've been mad if you called him elderly.

DAVID: [Laugh] Sorry, I just assumed. Thirties?

SUBJECT: No, maybe he was in his fifties.

DAVID: But he wasn't what you would call old.

SUBJECT: No.

DAVID: Was it one side of his face that was burned or his whole face?

SUBJECT: One side. One big burn on one side.

DAVID: Do you remember what he did before he passed away? Did he ever tell you?

SUBJECT: No.

DAVID: So, he didn't share a lot of information with you, but you could see him, and you would ask him things every once in a while, but he never really responded. Is that, right?

SUBJECT: Yeah.

DAVID: Now when you were in the bright light, and you don't remember where you went, but all of a sudden did you find yourself eventually somewhere?

SUBJECT: No, I just remember...

DAVID: What do you think happened to you?

SUBJECT: Well I guess I must have gone to Heaven, but I don't remember anything about it. I just remember the light and the feeling...

DAVID: You were in the light and what do you remember?

SUBJECT: Well I didn't feel hot anymore.

DAVID: So, your fever was gone.

SUBJECT: Yeah, it was kind of cool actually — the weather, the air, whatever it was, it felt cool.

DAVID: When did the light end for you?

SUBJECT: What?

DAVID: I'm sorry, I didn't mean end. But when you passed, all of a sudden he's there and says, "Wait and you'll see." You don't remember anything after he said that? Except you said your fever was gone.

SUBJECT: No. I don't remember.

DAVID: Did you see yourself coming out of your body when the light came?

SUBJECT: No, but I had a floating sensation, but I felt like that before, because of my fever.

DAVID: So, you're not sure where you went.

SUBJECT: I don't know.

DAVID: That's fine. Now let's go forward a little bit more in that life after you forgot where you went. We're not going to look at time, but when did you feel like you were somewhere else, when you weren't in that cottage anymore? When did you realize, you were somewhere else?

SUBJECT: I don't know.

DAVID: So, after that, you have no memories of anything.

SUBJECT: No.

DAVID: Okay... but you do remember light coming down. Did it feel like loving light?

SUBJECT: Yeah, I felt comforted.

Lieutenant Hertzof & the Age of Aquarius

This reading was conducted for a female subject. Her recall, knowledge and subsequent journey through the past life and her death afterward were recounted with great clarity and detail. Unexpectedly and without any prompting, at the end of the life journey as Lieutenant Hertzof, she shares the current cycle humankind has entered: "The Age of Aquarius."

The reading starts at the end of the hypnotic induction.

DAVID: So, I'm counting down from three to two. You know that you're safe and protected, floating along in your beautiful golden bubble of light. In your mind's eye, you will start to be able to see outside of this bubble, wanting to observe more of your journey. You're looking down over a beautiful, heavenly sea of flowers as you float above the ground, just floating along on the whispers of the winds of your lives.

As I count down to one, you feel the love, the protection, and the light from the golden energies that surround you. Wanting to explore more of your past and learn things in the process to help you on your way forward. Less uncertain, less fearful of the dark, knowing that you are always protected and loved on the entire journey.

So, as you hear my voice, totally alert in mind but relaxed, you're starting to see not only the field of flowers in your mind and the bubble you are floating in, but also you're going to relax enough to start to see some other things that are in your journey. Looking out of your protective bubble, I want you to think of a time you knew in the past. As you hear my voice, awake in mind, and not falling asleep, describe to me what your mind is showing you now, and I want you to tell us about it. Tell me what you see.

SUBJECT: [Light snoring sounds].

DAVID: What do you see?

SUBJECT: I see a tank.

DAVID: Okay, a tank. Like a water tank? What kind of tank?

SUBJECT: Like a military tank.

DAVID: A military tank. Is it... can you describe it to me a little?

SUBJECT: It's gray. It has a circle and a number painted on the side.

DAVID: Okay…

SUBJECT: Men are inside, and the top is open.

DAVID: And what kind of terrain are you crossing with this tank?

SUBJECT: The ground is wet. The sky is cloudy. There's smoke in the air.

DAVID: And where do you think this tank is right now?

SUBJECT: People are speaking another language.

DAVID: …and you're hearing them speak in the tank?

SUBJECT: I think they're speaking German.

DAVID: Do you see what year it is?

SUBJECT: I don't know.

DAVID: Can you give me the name of a town where this tank is, or near?

SUBJECT: We're near Brussels.

DAVID: Do you see yourself in the tank or are you just observing it?

SUBJECT: I'm just observing.

DAVID: Why is it important for you to observe and see this tank?

SUBJECT: [Pause] The men inside it are in my company.

DAVID: Do you remember what company that might be?

SUBJECT: [Long pause] I'm hearing two numbers…Third Reich, 18th battalion.

DAVID: Third Reich, 18th Battalion. Do you remember who is the leader or the general of this battalion or this regiment?

SUBJECT: His name starts with an M.

DAVID: Is he a General or what is his command?

SUBJECT: He's a general.

DAVID: Do you see in your mind who he reports to?

SUBJECT: No.

DAVID: And why are you moving toward Brussels? Do you know? Why are you in Brussels?

SUBJECT: We just captured it.

DAVID: Was everybody happy about that?

SUBJECT: Yes.

DAVID: Do you see now what year or month you captured Brussels? Do you see a month or what was it like that time of the year?

SUBJECT: It's cold.

DAVID: Do you remember what month? Was it before Christmas or after? Do you remember?

SUBJECT: I don't remember.

DAVID: Okay, but you know it was cold. When you think about it, do you see a month in your mind that might resonate with you?

SUBJECT: [Pause] There are still leaves on the trees.

DAVID: Are they turning brown or are they already brown?

SUBJECT: Yes.

DAVID: Could it have been before Christmas you think? Do you remember if you celebrated before or after the capture of Brussels, Christmas? [Pause] See any signs of celebration around Europe?

SUBJECT: I don't know.

DAVID: Now, how long were you in Brussels or how long was this tank there?

SUBJECT: Ten months.

DAVID: Were you part of this tank? What is your connection there?

SUBJECT: The men inside are in my company.

DAVID: Okay. You are just observing. Do you see yourself in Brussels?

SUBJECT: Yes.

DAVID: Can you tell me what you look like? What your uniform looks like?

SUBJECT: I'm tall. I have dark blond hair and a mustache and gray eyes.

DAVID: Do you remember your rank?

SUBJECT: I'm a lieutenant.

DAVID: Do you see, even if it is in German, do you see your first name? What pops into your head?

SUBJECT: [Long pause] I don't know my name.

DAVID: But you feel you were a Lieutenant.

SUBJECT: Yes.

DAVID: Do you remember when you enlisted? What year was that? How old were you? How old were you when you went to war to fight?

SUBJECT: Twenty-three.

DAVID: So, you were twenty-three years old. Do you remember what month you were born?

SUBJECT: No.

DAVID: Do you feel relaxed enough? Do you feel like you can see everything clearly? What did you do in Brussels? Was it a big fight or a little fight? Was it easier than you thought going in?

SUBJECT: The town was smoking.

DAVID: Was the town Brussels or one right outside of Brussels?

SUBJECT: Outside of Brussels.

DAVID: Do you remember looking at a map as a Lieutenant? Do you see where that town was on the map in relation to Brussels?

Was it circled red somewhere on the map, somewhere near Brussels? What did that town start with? What was the first letter?

SUBJECT: It starts with 'I.'

DAVID: The town started with an 'I.' Do you remember if it was north of Brussels or south?

SUBJECT: Southwest.

DAVID: Southwest of Brussels. Do you remember how many clicks or kilometers from Brussels it was roughly?

SUBJECT: No.

DAVID: Do you know how many miles it was?

SUBJECT: No.

DAVID: Do you remember what kind of tank you were observing or with? What kind of tank was it? Does it have a name?

SUBJECT: It has a name. It's a name that's well known today. Panzer? Panzer.

DAVID: Was it made by Germans in Germany?

SUBJECT: Yes.

DAVID: Do you remember how much it weighed roughly? How big was it?

SUBJECT: It was a newly developed machine for war. It was powerful. Panzer means armor.

DAVID: Did you ever get to ride in the tank?

SUBJECT: Yes.

DAVID: Was it fun?

SUBJECT: Yes.

DAVID: Do you remember what kind of gun it had and what size of projectiles it shot?

SUBJECT: It killed anything in its path.

DAVID: Do you remember how far the bullets would go when you guys would shoot at other tanks?

SUBJECT: Over fifty yards and much farther than that.

DAVID: So easily over fifty yards? Now as you are looking at that life as a Lieutenant and you said you were in this little town.... Do you see the name of the little town that started with an 'I'? Do you see that now?

SUBJECT: There is a 'S' and an 'N' in the name.

DAVID: So 'I" 'S' and 'N'. Were those the first three letters or what do you see?

SUBJECT: I don't know.

DAVID: That's okay...you said it was kind of cold...there were still leaves on the trees, it was cold though.

SUBJECT: Mhm.

DAVID: Did it feel like November, December, or October? Do you remember?

SUBJECT: November.

DAVID: Okay. Middle of November or end, when you think you rode into that town?

SUBJECT: We arrived in the beginning of November.

DAVID: So pretty much the beginning of November. And you are pretty sure as you think about it in your mind's eye, and what you hear in your mind...is that the town maybe started with an 'I' but also had an 'N' and an 'S.' Was it two syllables you think or just one?

SUBJECT: Two.

DAVID: So, two syllables?

SUBJECT: Yes.

DAVID: Was it in French or what was the language?

SUBJECT: I don't know.

DAVID: You didn't recognize it?

SUBJECT: No.

DAVID: Did you see any letters besides 'I', 'N', and 'S'? Any others you can tell?

SUBJECT: 'R'.

DAVID: Which one?

SUBJECT: The letter 'R'.

DAVID: So, there was an 'I', and 'N', 'S', and 'R'. And what other vowels were there?

SUBJECT: I can't tell. The map is torn.

DAVID: I understand. Can you see any other consonants or not really?

SUBJECT: [Sigh] No.

DAVID: That's okay. Now, let's go forward a bit. You said you stayed in Brussels or outside of Brussels in this little town for ten months. Is that correct?

SUBJECT: Yes.

DAVID: And you think you were around the age of twenty-three at the time. Right?

SUBJECT: Yes.

DAVID: Do you see your name now? Your first name? What letters were in your first name?

SUBJECT: [Deep breathing]

DAVID: And I want you just to hear my voice and no other noises. Go ahead.

SUBJECT: My first name isn't on my uniform, just the first letter.

DAVID: And what was the first letter, do you remember?

SUBJECT: 'K'

DAVID: So, on your nametag, when you are staring at your uniform, as an observer, give me the last name. Look at the nametag. Take your time.

SUBJECT: It starts with an 'H'.

DAVID: Starts with an 'H'. What is the next letter? What is the vowel? Is there a vowel next? What did it sound like in your mind if somebody addressed you, and you turned around suddenly and saw it?

SUBJECT: [Pause] The name Hertz. H-E-R-T-Z.

DAVID: So, you think that was your name or was there more to the name? Was it one syllable?

SUBJECT: It was something like Hertz, but I think that's just the way that name sounds. Hertzof, or... Hertzel.

DAVID: So, something with the first syllable being Hertz...

SUBJECT: Yeah.

DAVID: Now let's just look at that second syllable and forget about Hertz. What does that second syllable sound like?

SUBJECT: -off.

DAVID: Say it again.

SUBJECT: -off.

DAVID: So, like Hertzof — O-F-F?

SUBJECT: O.F.

DAVID: So, you think your last name had two syllables?

SUBJECT: Yeah.

DAVID: And the first name, what did that start with again? Give me that first letter of your name again.

SUBJECT: 'K'.

DAVID: So, it felt like your name, and correct me if I'm wrong, that it might have been K. Hertzof.

SUBJECT: Yes.

DAVID: Does that sound right? And you think you were a Lieutenant in this battalion. Is that correct?

SUBJECT: Yes.

DAVID: And how old are you again roughly?

SUBJECT: Twenty-three.

DAVID: Were you married?

SUBJECT: Yes.

DAVID: Did you write letters to your wife while you were away?

SUBJECT: Yes.

DAVID: And do you remember, what was her name?

SUBJECT: [Pause] Laurel.

DAVID: How do you say her name again?

SUBJECT: Laurel.

DAVID: Laurel, like L-A-U-R-E-L?

SUBJECT: Yeah.

DAVID: Did she have a middle name by any chance? Do you remember any nicknames or middle names?

SUBJECT: [Long pause].

DAVID: Any coming to mind?

SUBJECT: [Pause] No.

DAVID: Okay. Did you have children?

SUBJECT: Yes.

DAVID: And let's think about that for a moment as you watch them play. How many children did you and Laurel have?

SUBJECT: We had two sons.

DAVID: Two sons. Now when you were twenty-three, how old was Laurel roughly? Was she older or younger than you?

SUBJECT: She was eighteen.

DAVID: So, when you were twenty-three, she was eighteen years old. How old were you when you got married?

SUBJECT: [Pause] Twenty-two.

DAVID: So, you had been married a year before you left, is that correct?

SUBJECT: Yeah.

DAVID: Now do you remember what year you were married? What year was that? What was the wedding date? What month was it?

SUBJECT: [Pause with deep breathing] I don't know.

DAVID: Did you get married in a church or did you get married at home? Where did you get married? Do you see the wedding?

SUBJECT: Yes.

DAVID: Good. Let's go to that wedding for a moment then we will go back to the children. Looking at that wedding, what town did you get married in?

SUBJECT: I don't remember the name.

DAVID: Do you remember what religion the church was?

SUBJECT: Catholic.

DAVID: So, it was a Catholic church and you had a Catholic priest do the wedding ceremony?

SUBJECT: Yeah.

DAVID: Do you see your parents there with you as you're getting married?

SUBJECT: No.

DAVID: They weren't at the wedding?

SUBJECT: No.

DAVID: Now as just an observer, did they pass away?

SUBJECT: Yeah.

DAVID: And what was your father's name that passed away, do you remember?

SUBJECT: His name was Derek.

DAVID: Derek. And what was his last name?

SUBJECT: Hmm.

DAVID: Was it the same as yours?

SUBJECT: Hertzof.

DAVID: Say that again.

SUBJECT: [Pause] Hertzof.

DAVID: Hertzof. And do you remember your mother's first name? What was her name?

SUBJECT: [Pause] Margarite.

DAVID: Margarite. What were your children's names? Let's go look at your children. What were their names and how old were they when you left for war at twenty-three?

SUBJECT: Two-and-a-half and less than a year.

DAVID: Do you remember those boys' names? [Pause] What was one of the son's names? Who was the oldest?

SUBJECT: John.

DAVID: John was the oldest. So, he was about two-and-a-half when you left. Is that true?

SUBJECT: Yes.

DAVID: What did you and your wife name the younger one? Do you remember?

SUBJECT: His name started with an 'R'.

DAVID: With an 'R'. Was it a long word or one syllable do you think?

SUBJECT: It was not long. Raul.

DAVID: It was like Raul?

SUBJECT: Yes.

DAVID: Or something like that? And how would you spell that?

SUBJECT: No, Reif. R-E-I-F.

DAVID: Reif, what a nice name. And he was pretty young when you left wasn't he?

SUBJECT: Yeah.

DAVID: Did you miss your boys and your wife?

SUBJECT: Yeah.

DAVID: Good. Now why did you leave? Did you have to leave? Was it required that you leave to go to war or did you want to stay with your family? Did you think it was the right thing to do? What was your mindset when you decided to leave? When you were told to leave?

SUBJECT: I was doing my job.

DAVID: So, you were doing your job. Was it a job that you felt was for the country, or what was it for?

SUBJECT: Our boss told us what our job was, and we did our job.

DAVID: And who was your boss? Do you remember his name? Who was ahead of you as a Lieutenant? Who is your immediate supervisor? What was his name? What was his rank?

SUBJECT: I don't remember his name.

DAVID: Did you and your friends in the tank call him something, like some name that he probably wouldn't have liked or not? Do you remember?

SUBJECT: We didn't call him names.

DAVID: So, everybody was pretty proper and did their job. Is that right?

SUBJECT: Yeah.

DAVID: Did you go home after the war, or what happened?

SUBJECT: I didn't go home.

DAVID: Now you're just observing. I want you to just observe and not get emotionally involved, we're just looking at that life with you as a Lieutenant, correct?

SUBJECT: [Sharp inhale] Mhmm…yes.

DAVID: And I want you to just relax. And what was your last name again?

SUBJECT: Hertzof.

DAVID: Now you're just going to view that life. You're not getting involved. You're not going to get emotional. You're just observing. That life is gone. It is done and that is okay. And I want you to tell me, as you see yourself, where did you go from that town outside of Brussels after the ten months were up. Where did you go after that?

SUBJECT: [Pause] We traveled south.

DAVID: So, you traveled south. That's good. Now let's go on that journey again together. We're leaving the small town outside of Brussels where you have been for the previous ten months. And we are going south, just kind of going along. How many tanks were in your battalion do you think?

SUBJECT: Thirteen.

DAVID: Thirteen. And was your tank in the middle of the thirteen, or sort of in the front or the back? Where was your tank in that line of thirteen as you look down at it?

SUBJECT: There were two ahead of us.

DAVID: Two ahead of you. Were you riding in the tank at the time when you were going south, or did you get there another way?

SUBJECT: I was in the tank.

DAVID: So, you were in the tank with them. Were you a tank commander or who ran the tank?

SUBJECT: Another man.

DAVID: Was he pretty good, the other man, your friend?

SUBJECT: My colleague.

DAVID: Your colleague. Did you not like him too much, or how did you get along with the other men in the tank?

SUBJECT: He was a wise-ass.

DAVID: So, the tank commander was a wise-ass, right?

SUBJECT: He thought he was the commander, but he just drove the thing.

DAVID: He thought he was kind of cool overall?

SUBJECT: Yeah.

DAVID: What was his name? What was his first name?

SUBJECT: It started with a 'P'.

DAVID: Started with a 'P'.

SUBJECT: Phillip.

DAVID: Great, Phillip. And what was his last name, when you looked at his tag or just kind of thought about it. What was his last name? What did it start with? Can you remember?

SUBJECT: I can't see his name.

DAVID: That's okay. How many people are in the tank with you? How many other guys besides you and Phillip?

SUBJECT: Three.

DAVID: Three other guys. And what were their names? Do you remember? Any other names? What were those guys' names? [Pause] Do you have any buddies on the tank you were closer to?

SUBJECT: Jeremy.

DAVID: So, Jeremy, was he a pretty good guy?

SUBJECT: Yes.

DAVID: So, he is a good friend of yours, is that what you are telling me?

SUBJECT: He was an honorable man.

DAVID: He was what?

SUBJECT: He was an honorable man.

DAVID: An honorable man. And what was Jeremy's last name?

SUBJECT: Buchanan.

DAVID: What's that?

SUBJECT: Buchanan.

DAVID: Was he German?

SUBJECT: Yes.

DAVID: He was German, but his name was Jeremy Buchanan like the U.S. President Buchanan?

SUBJECT: Yes.

DAVID: Do you remember Jeremy's middle initial? Did he have one or do you not remember?

SUBJECT: I don't know.

DAVID: What was Jeremy's job on the tank? What did he do while Phillip was driving?

SUBJECT: He operated the machine gun.

DAVID: He operated the machine gun. What kind of bullets did it shoot? What was the caliber of those bullets? [Pause] Were they big? Were they long? What would have Lieutenant Hertzof thought when he's looking at those bullets, as he's holding them in his hands or holding that belt in his hands? How long were those bullets when you looked at those? Were they three inches, four inches, one inch? What size do you think those bullets were?

SUBJECT: About three inches long.

DAVID: Now as a lieutenant, what was Phillip's rank as the driver? What was his rank? [Pause] Do you remember? Did you out-rank him? Or were you guys both lieutenants?

SUBJECT: He was lower than me.

DAVID: He was lower than you?

SUBJECT: Yes.

DAVID: So lower than a lieutenant. What was Jeremy?

SUBJECT: A Colonel.

DAVID: Oh, you're saying Jeremy was a Colonel?

SUBJECT: Yes.

DAVID: So, Jeremy who was riding in your tank was a Colonel. And his last name was what? Jeremy Buchanan? Is that what you thought?

SUBJECT: His name is B-U.

DAVID: Say that again?

SUBJECT: His last name was B-U.

DAVID: And what was the rest?

SUBJECT: Sounded like "cannon" but… I don't remember how it was spelled.

DAVID: But it was different than what we know as Buchanan, is that correct?

SUBJECT: Yeah.

DAVID: And he was a Colonel, is that what you remember?

SUBJECT: Yeah.

DAVID: Was it unusual to have a Colonel riding in your tank or was that pretty common? Was he the only Colonel in those tanks?

SUBJECT: He was the only Colonel.

DAVID: So, he was allowed... He rode in your tank is that correct?

SUBJECT: Sometimes.

DAVID: So, he was the only Colonel of those thirteen tanks. Is that correct?

SUBJECT: Yeah.

DAVID: And he picked your tank and that was the big moment when he rode in your tank, is that right?

SUBJECT: [Pause] He did what he wanted.

DAVID: Was it nice having him on board or did he make you a little nervous when you were going south?

SUBJECT: No, he was a reassuring person.

DAVID: So, he made you feel safer having him in there because he's a pretty nice, honorable man. Is that correct?

SUBJECT: Yeah.

DAVID: Do you remember what Jeremy told you, the Colonel, did he tell you how far from Brussels you would be going when you headed south? Did he share that information with you?

SUBJECT: About a day's ride.

DAVID: A day's ride by tank, is that correct?

SUBJECT: Yeah.

DAVID: So, you went south, and you left that little town that started with an 'I'... with thirteen tanks, right?

SUBJECT: Yeah.

DAVID: How far did you go and how fast were you going south? Do you remember? Was it kind of slow or maybe fifteen, twenty clicks just to be safe? What was the speed roughly?

SUBJECT: We were not in a hurry.

DAVID: You were just taking your time?

SUBJECT: Yeah.

DAVID: Were there concerns about enemy fire coming at you or something?

SUBJECT: Yeah.

DAVID: Was there a very big presence of American troops there at the time that you were a little concerned about?

SUBJECT: [Inhale deeply] American and British.

DAVID: So American and British troops, okay. Did you lose some friends... not looking at yourself yet, but did you lose some other tanks in the process trying to make that ride south?

SUBJECT: We were ambushed.

DAVID: And how far south were you ambushed? Do you remember?

SUBJECT: We were at the border.

[The subject's breathing started to increase. I reiterated, "You are only observing the life."]

DAVID: And you were attacked near the border, is that what you are telling me?

SUBJECT: Yeah.

DAVID: Was it almost right at the border, like, "Oh my God, this is not good"?

SUBJECT: Yeah. Everything happened so fast.

DAVID: Did you make it to the border at least or do you not remember?

SUBJECT: I don't remember.

DAVID: You just knew it was coming up, is that correct?

SUBJECT: Yeah.

DAVID: Did maybe Phillip in the tank or someone say, "The border is only about a couple of clicks away," or something like that?

SUBJECT: Yeah.

DAVID: Did Phillip tell you how far away it was, or he didn't know because your tank was following the tank in front of it?

SUBJECT: He told me, but I don't remember.

DAVID: Now I want you to just observe, don't get involved, emotionally, we're just observing. Can you do that for me?

SUBJECT: Yeah. [Heavier breathing]

[Subject was starting to get more anxious, I reiterated, "You are just observing, and you are not getting emotionally involved." This approach usually produces more clarity and focus, and keeps them from getting lost in the tragedy they are experiencing.]

DAVID: I want you to just relax. You are protected. We are just looking at that life, and you are not getting emotional. Can you do that?

SUBJECT: Yeah.

DAVID: [Softly] Tell me what happened. Who attacked you?

SUBJECT: We were pinned down by enemy fire. They must have known…our coordinates. We…we didn't last long.

DAVID: Did they take out all thirteen tanks or what? Do you remember?

SUBJECT: They blew up five.

DAVID: They blew up five of those tanks. And then there was what, eight other tanks that didn't get blown up. Is that correct?

SUBJECT: Yeah.

DAVID: And what happened to those people in the tanks? What happened to them? Did they jump out or run? How did that work? What did you see? And remember, you're just observing.

SUBJECT: They stopped, and they unloaded their machine gun fire, but we ran out of ammo before they did.

DAVID: And who was shooting that machine gun on your tank, do you remember? Who was that soldier again?

[Asking the subject similar questions later into the regression verifies the recall on very specific details. The subject's fast and accurate recall is notable. At this stage, they are deep enough in a super-conscious state to fully embody the person they're describing. The state the subject is currently in would be no different than your discussing your present life with someone.]

SUBJECT: That was Jeremy.

DAVID: So, Jeremy, and you liked Jeremy, is that correct?

SUBJECT: Yeah.

DAVID: So, he was doing the machine gun and all of a sudden your bullets ran out, is that what you're telling me?

SUBJECT: Yeah.

DAVID: And then what happened inside your tank? What happened then? What do you remember? And we are just observing.

SUBJECT: I remember the smell of gasoline.

DAVID: The smell of gasoline. And why was the smell so much stronger now?

SUBJECT: They shot our fuel tank.

DAVID: Now do you remember, was it the British or the Americans or both? Was it a group effort or just one or the other? Did you ever hear about that later?

SUBJECT: [Deep breathing—getting a little emotional] It was the British.

DAVID: Okay, and how many tanks did they have compared to your thirteen?

SUBJECT: I don't know.

DAVID: Because it happened fast, is that right? Now what happened when your gas tank blew up, and you are just observing, what happened then? When you smelled that gas, take me through that.

SUBJECT: In a matter of seconds, the interior was full of fire.

DAVID: Oh, now let's just observe. What happened to everyone then?

SUBJECT: Our tank exploded.

DAVID: Now can you just observe and not get emotional? Can we do that together?

SUBJECT: Yes.

DAVID: Knowing you're protected, right? What happened next? It exploded then what happened to Lieutenant Hertzof? What do you see? Just observing. How do you see yourself?

SUBJECT: [Sharp inhale, pause]

DAVID: Just observe, and don't get emotional. What happened?

SUBJECT: [Deep breath, anxious swallow] My leg was blown off, and my body was thrown. I hit something and broke my jaw, and I don't remember anything after that.

DAVID: Okay. When the tank was on fire, let me ask you this, did Lieutenant Hertzof try to get out of the tank while it was on fire?

SUBJECT: No, everything happened too fast.

DAVID: So, you were you still in the tank when it blew up?

SUBJECT: I was still in the tank.

DAVID: But you remember that you got thrown around the tank and somehow your leg was blown off in the process. Is that correct? And then you hit your jaw. Is that what you remember?

SUBJECT: Yeah.

DAVID: And then what? It was just over?

SUBJECT: That's it.

DAVID: Which leg was it? Was it your left or your right leg?

SUBJECT: My left leg.

DAVID: Now you are just observing. Was everyone else killed in the tank too? Jeremy, and Phillip, and everyone?

SUBJECT: I could hear them screaming.

DAVID: Were you already gone before they died? Do you remember? Or was everyone about the same time?

SUBJECT: I don't know.

DAVID: Your leg was blown off and you hit your jaw, and that's all you remember from the tank. Is that correct?

SUBJECT: Yeah.

DAVID: Now I just want you to observe. What did you see next?

SUBJECT: Nothing.

DAVID: Was it just dark? Or was it light? What was it?

SUBJECT: There was nothing.

DAVID: So, there was just kind of a void of nothing. No tanks, no noise, no smells, no light, just nothing. Is that correct?

SUBJECT: Yes.

DAVID: Were you scared at that point realizing that everything was nothing? What were your thoughts at that point? What do you remember consciously when you were there? Were you scared, or didn't care, or didn't have time to think about it, or what happened? How long was your nothing?

SUBJECT: [Pause] I don't know.

DAVID: But there was nothing. That means no light, no dark, no gray. Or was it gray?

SUBJECT: There was nothing.

DAVID: Did you see anybody else in the nothing or were you by yourself?

SUBJECT: I was alone.

DAVID: You were totally alone. Now let's think together. Let's go forward a little bit longer, just a little bit longer. How long were you in nothing?

SUBJECT: I don't know.

DAVID: Let's not look so much at time. Let's try not to think of time, because that is where it is getting a little hard to quantify. Let's go to the end of nothing. Not thinking of time or hours, or days or weeks or months, tell me what you saw at the end of nothing. What did you finally come across? What did you finally see after nothing?

SUBJECT: A pool of light.

DAVID: A pool of light. Was it a big pool or a small pool? Tell me about that pool.

SUBJECT: It's about the size of a large pond.

DAVID: So, you found yourself in nothing and then after a time, you don't know how long that was, suddenly, a pool of light came in? Did it come in all of a sudden or did it just gradually come in to where you were?

SUBJECT: It was sudden.

DAVID: So, a pool of light came in sudden. What did that pool tell you, or what did you feel, what do you remember when you saw that pool of light?

SUBJECT: I was submerged in it.

DAVID: So, you felt submerged in this pool of light. Is that correct?

SUBJECT: Yes.

DAVID: Describe that to me.

SUBJECT: It was warm.

DAVID: It was warm. What else?

SUBJECT: [Pause] It felt like things were vibrating.

DAVID: Go on.

SUBJECT: [Pause] I could see myself again.

DAVID: Okay.

SUBJECT: But my leg wasn't blown off.

DAVID: Continue.

SUBJECT: My jaw wasn't broken.

DAVID: Keep going. Then what happened? You saw yourself. Were you happy then? Did you feel whole again? What did you feel?

SUBJECT: I felt intact, but I felt sad.

DAVID: Why were you sad?

SUBJECT: [Pause] I wept for my sins.

DAVID: You wept for your what?

SUBJECT: For my sins.

DAVID: And what sins did you see that you committed? Tell me about some of those. And remember it's okay. What sins did you commit?

SUBJECT: Murder.

DAVID: Murder. And whom did you murder?

SUBJECT: Anyone our boss told us to.

DAVID: So, you realized in the pool of light, seeing yourself whole again that what your boss told you to do, killing another human being was wrong and a sin. Is that correct?

SUBJECT: [Anxious swallow] Yes.

DAVID: And what other sins did you commit?

SUBJECT: [Pause] I envied, and I lusted for power.

DAVID: Did you want to be more than a lieutenant?

SUBJECT: Yes.

DAVID: And how did you think you would get there? Would it take more murder? Give me some background on what you did. You lusted for more power. Tell me about that.

SUBJECT: I was intelligent, but I wasn't a good man. I was conniving.

DAVID: What else?

SUBJECT: I was willing to do whatever I had to do to the detriment of others.

DAVID: Keep going. What else did you realize about yourself?

SUBJECT: [Pause, sharp inhale] Even though I loved my family… I would have killed them if I were ordered to.

DAVID: Wow. Was that one of the hardest things of all? Did that really hurt when you realized the wrongness of that?

SUBJECT: I wept for my sins.

DAVID: And did you weep alone in this pool of light or did you weep in front of someone else?

SUBJECT: I was alone physically, but I felt presence with me.

DAVID: And give me some idea, who do you think that presence was?

SUBJECT: It was God.

DAVID: God. It was God you wept in front of, confessing your sins and realizing what you had done. Is that correct?

SUBJECT: Yeah.

DAVID: And what else can you tell me? What did God do when you wept in front of him? Did he say anything or what happened after that? What was his response?

SUBJECT: God touched my shoulder, and he told me that it was forgiven.

DAVID: Was that pool of light… did that feel like what we know as heaven to you?

SUBJECT: I don't know, but anything was heaven compared to the nothing.

DAVID: Did that nothing, that absolute nothing place you were, did you think in your mind, with what you knew as Lieutenant Hertzof, did you think maybe that was what they talk about as being hell? What were your thoughts on that?

SUBJECT: That was hell.

DAVID: ...So why did the pool of light come for Lieutenant Hertzof? What did God say to you? Why did he finally come for you into the nothingness?

SUBJECT: Well, in church we were taught that you had to do penance and then you had to atone. The nothing was penance, but I would still have to atone for that life.

DAVID: Is that what God told you? You had to atone?

SUBJECT: Yeah.

DAVID: And how would Lieutenant Hertzof.... let's go forward a little bit more. Now you are just observing, that's all. How long did God stay with you then, and talk to you? What did it feel like?

SUBJECT: I spent a long time there.

DAVID: ...and how long did you weep? Do you remember?

SUBJECT: It felt like an age.

DAVID: It felt like what again?

SUBJECT: It felt like an age.

DAVID: Now what is an age? Can you describe what an age would be, let's say in Earth years, today? How long is an age?

SUBJECT: It felt like a thousand years.

DAVID: So, it felt like a thousand years and that's what's known as an age?

SUBJECT: Yes.

DAVID: Is that a unit of measurement in heaven or what you thought was hell to account for a certain time? An age? How did you know that? Did that just come to you? Or how did you ever hear of that?

SUBJECT: It was from a book.

DAVID: What book is that? Did you learn that in school or in church back in Germany?

SUBJECT: It was something a priest said.

DAVID: So, it felt like an age, or a thousand years. Is that how long you wept?

SUBJECT: Yes.

DAVID: And after you were done weeping, and God told you that you were forgiven, what did God say is beyond that? Can you share that?

SUBJECT: He said a life for a life.

DAVID: And what did he mean by that?

SUBJECT: That only by living on the other end of that violence... only by learning... could I undo the evils that I had committed.

DAVID: So, was it like a karmic type thing that he told you? A life-for-a-life?

SUBJECT: I suppose you could call it that.

DAVID: Now what did it mean? You would have to learn what? By taking lives, what would you have to do next? Give me a little background.

SUBJECT: To kill is to become... something other than human. You revoke your humanity by taking the life of someone else and the only way to atone for that is to learn on the receiving end of that same violence in another life.

DAVID: And God spoke to you and told you that. Is that what you are telling me now? That is what you learned?

SUBJECT: Yes. That is what I learned.

DAVID: So, even though your boss told you to hurt others, that is not an excuse to kill, is that correct?

SUBJECT: Yes.

DAVID: You still have to recognize, regardless of who tells you to do things, that if you take another's life, God doesn't look at someone telling you to do that as an excuse. Is that what you're telling me today?

SUBJECT: Yes.

DAVID: Okay. So, has God ever told people to kill, or what about all of that in the Old Testament? What can you share about that? Was God ever vengeful? Or you're not sure? How did he come off to you?

SUBJECT: God said, "Vengeance is mine."

DAVID: Okay. But that doesn't mean human, is that correct or not? From your understanding.

SUBJECT: God said, "Vengeance is mine," the implication being that humans have to stay out of his way.

DAVID: Does God ever... When you first encountered God, you felt he was that pool of light that engulfed you, is that correct? That lake of light?

SUBJECT: Yes.

DAVID: Was there anyone else that was with him in that lake of light to meet you? Was there Jesus or anybody else we know as ascended masters?

SUBJECT: No.

DAVID: So, God came to Lieutenant Hertzof in that pool of light. And it was God, is that correct?

SUBJECT: Yes.

DAVID: Now when God spoke to you and said he forgave you, but you would have to atone for taking others' lives, is that something that will play out in future lives? Do you feel that is what your interpretation was?

SUBJECT: He said, "It's forgiven, but you still have to atone."

DAVID: Now that he told you that, did you feel relieved that you were forgiven by God? Did you feel relieved to be out of that void, that hell you mentioned?

SUBJECT: Yes.

DAVID: Did you stay in that pool of light for a while, that pool of love and light? Where did you go from there as that soul, Lieutenant Hertzof? Where did you go? Do you remember where you went?

SUBJECT: I don't remember.

DAVID: So, let's go forward a little more. Now when God left, and you were there, and you see yourself whole again, let's think about that for a bit. Did you see others eventually? Did you see houses? What did you see?

SUBJECT: I don't remember.

[I could sense the subject was understandably upset after reviewing that life and was starting to shut down. Her reticence to provide further details was apparent after my last two questions. I felt it best to move past that life at this stage.]

DAVID: Would you like to not think any more about Lieutenant Hertzof? Knowing he's okay and he's forgiven.

SUBJECT: Yes.

DAVID: Okay, let's float away from that life. Erase all of the feelings, all of the thoughts. And let's think about something else.

Let's forget all about that as you move forward in your bubble, as you coast along. Can you do that with me?

SUBJECT: Yes.

DAVID: Now let's think as you float along, back over that sea of flowers away from everything you just thought about. Forgetting all of those memories and moving on. Your mind's eye still open, looking ahead, seeing the sea of flowers in front of you. Moving along in this golden bubble, knowing the angels are with you. And you are going to move on and forget about any other pasts right now. Can you see that field of flowers as we float along?

SUBJECT: Yes.

DAVID: What colors do you see in the field? What pretty flowers do you like and see?

SUBJECT: I see Black-Eyed Susans.

DAVID: Okay. What others?

SUBJECT: Day lilies.

DAVID: And how far above those flowers do you think you are as you're floating along?

SUBJECT: Two feet.

DAVID: So, you are floating right above them, is that right?

SUBJECT: Umm…yes.

DAVID: So, float along above the flowers. And as you are floating above the flowers, looking at the beautiful flowers beneath you and very close, continue floating along. Just floating along. Feeling so good, feeling so happy. All of the stress and negative thoughts from that life are draining out of your body. Knowing that we're immortal, that was one life of many you've had, and life goes on. Can you do that with me?

SUBJECT: Yes.

DAVID: So, as you're floating along, you are going to move on and on. And you are going to picture an earlier time. Can we do that together?

SUBJECT: Yes.

DAVID: In your mind's eye, stop for a moment just hovering over these flowers, and you are opening your mind's eye even more in the bubble. Knowing you are resting above this beautiful, safe field of flowers. Just stop here for a moment, just rocking back and forth on the breezes of your life and your journey. Above this beautiful field of flowers. Can you do that with me?

SUBJECT: Yes.

DAVID: Let's think about those little freckles above your eyelid. Those three little freckles. We're not going to think about anything else. What do those freckles symbolize? Do they mean anything? Are they from another life too, or what are your thoughts on it?

SUBJECT: They are a constellation.

DAVID: Now you're just going to relax and let's look at them together. Just relax, knowing that angels and archangels protect you and no darkness or evil can come into your circle. You are protected in your bubble of golden light. Now what constellation do they represent? It's not coming from -----------'s conscious but coming from your subconscious in the bubble. What do they represent?

SUBJECT: Orion's Belt.

DAVID: Say that again please.

SUBJECT: Orion's Belt.

DAVID: They represent Orion's Belt. Now why is that important? Tell me about that. What does that mean?

SUBJECT: It has to do with the constellations during the month that I was born.

DAVID: And was Orion in the house when you were born? Is that what you're telling me?

SUBJECT: Yes.

DAVID: Were there other constellations in your birth sign or birth chart?

SUBJECT: I don't know.

DAVID: But it was something that was important. That Orion was in your birth chart. Is that correct?

SUBJECT: Yes.

DAVID: Is there anything else you want to tell me about that? Any other significance?

SUBJECT: The Age of Aquarius. We are in the age.

DAVID: The Age of Aquarius. Is that what you've been told?

SUBJECT: It's in Mercury.

DAVID: Say that again please.

SUBJECT: It's in Mercury.

DAVID: Are we entering what's known as the Age of Aquarius, now?

SUBJECT: Yes.

DAVID: And what can you tell me about that age, as you are floating along in your bubble. What can you feel about that age? What can you see?

SUBJECT: Heightened creativity, innovation, an age of growth and progress.

DAVID: Describe that progress. What do you mean by progress?

SUBJECT: Psychic awareness.

DAVID: So, the Age of Aquarius means progress in psychic awareness among humans?

SUBJECT: Yes.

DAVID: All humans or just some humans? Give me some background on that.

SUBJECT: Humans born in the Aquarius sign.

DAVID: So, for humans born in an Aquarius sign, you see that they will have more heightened awareness or psychic abilities, is that correct?

SUBJECT: Yes.

DAVID: Are they the only ones on the zodiac chart, or who else? What other groups or months? What do you see?

SUBJECT: It's different for every sign.

DAVID: Okay. But does it feel to you, when you look at those twelve signs, for the twelve months of the year, and not looking at this as ------------, just looking at it as what you are being told. What you feel in your subconscious as you float above the flowers. Stop for a moment, just thinking. Are those born in the sign of Aquarius, are they going to be more psychic than the other eleven signs, in your opinion?

SUBJECT: In this age... yes.

DAVID: Give me some ideas of what might happen with these Aquarians. What are they bringing for us, for mankind?

SUBJECT: They're going to be able to cross the barrier.

DAVID: Cross the barrier. What barrier is that? Can you tell me that?

SUBJECT: That which separates us from the Divine.

DAVID: Now, besides Aquarians, who else will be able to cross that barrier?

SUBJECT: Anyone who's tuned in.

DAVID: And how does one become tuned in? What does that mean?

SUBJECT: Has to do with intuition, looking inward.

DAVID: Say that again please.

SUBJECT: Looking inward.

DAVID: Now how do you know this? Have you heard this from your subconscious, the other side, or how do you know to look inward?

SUBJECT: I just know.

DAVID: So, you just know that's how to cross the barrier. Is that what you're telling me now?

SUBJECT: Yes.

DAVID: Now how do we look inward? How do we do that? What can a person do to look inward? Can you explain that to me? What do we need to do?

[Though I had been meditating for quite some time and was well aware what *inward* meant, I wanted the subject to share her thoughts and interpretation of what "going inward" meant to her. I felt the subject was in a very deep, super-conscious state at this time based on her responses. Providing information that was not requested or prompted on the current age that mankind has entered shows how deep her hypnotic state was. A super-conscious state is the deepest state a person in a hypnotic trance can experience. At this state, one is tapping into their divine selves and profound information often results.]

SUBJECT: Meditation. We have to recognize the interconnectivity of all living things.

DAVID: Gotcha, and then what? What do we do next? Or what happens if we can't recognize that, then how do we go from there?

SUBJECT: We have to transcend our Earthly shortcomings.

DAVID: All right, tell me more about that.

SUBJECT: We have to give up the things that are not important.

DAVID: And what would those be? Give me some examples.

SUBJECT: We have to let go of greed, the things that we hunger for that don't feed our soul. We have to sacrifice.

DAVID: We have to what?

SUBJECT: To sacrifice.

DAVID: And how do we sacrifice?

SUBJECT: We try to become as much, as much like God, as much like Jesus, as we can.

DAVID: And who else would be up in that area besides Jesus? Who else that has laid a way for some people? Who comes to mind in other religions that might have helped others find the way?

SUBJECT: There are many people who have found the way.

DAVID: And this is what you feel is the time of the Age of Aquarius. Is that correct?

SUBJECT: Yes.

DAVID: And how long will that time last in earth years? What feels good for a number for you?

SUBJECT: It's hard to say, but I think it will be the next forty years.

DAVID: The next what?

SUBJECT: The next forty years.

DAVID: So, you think over the next forty years, that the Age of Aquarius will become more of the view for everyone.

SUBJECT: Yes.

DAVID: Or just the ones that go with it? What are your thoughts on that?

SUBJECT: There will be leaders that come forth.

DAVID: Say that again, please.

SUBJECT: There will be leaders from every nation.

DAVID: They'll be arriving, you're saying?

SUBJECT: They will come forth, and many of them will be under the Aquarius sign.

DAVID: Will Jesus come forth as well, or will his spirit be with all of the leaders?

SUBJECT: This will happen before Jesus comes again.

DAVID: Okay. Will they help pave the way for Jesus to come again?

SUBJECT: Yes.

DAVID: Like John the Baptist, perhaps? Is that what you're telling me here?

SUBJECT: Yes.

DAVID: And will the leaders be in all nations?

SUBJECT: Yes.

DAVID: And what can you tell me about these leaders? Where are they coming from? Or are they here now?

SUBJECT: They are here, or they are not yet here.

DAVID: So, for the next forty years, there will be some that come, some that are already here, and some that are yet to be born?

SUBJECT: Yes.

DAVID: Will they be on every nation on Earth?

SUBJECT: Yes.

DAVID: Got it. Will they help lead or teach those that have not yet found the way inward?

SUBJECT: They will have their followings, respectively.

DAVID: Tell me about some of these followings. Are they going to be held in churches, religious structures or buildings? Where will these followings be held?

SUBJECT: They're not confined to any building.

DAVID: Now are these answers coming from help that you are getting from the Divine side?

SUBJECT: I just know.

DAVID: And how is our progress going now when we look at wars? When we look at the Middle East and we see a lot of separation today with Christians fighting with Muslims and soldiers and the innocent getting hurt — where do we stand on global separation? Where does the human condition stand right now?

SUBJECT: It's always darkest before dawn.

DAVID: So is this considered... How many years of darkness do you think before we enter the Age of Aquarius more fully and realize its glory?

SUBJECT: I don't know. Human free will dictates, and free will is never static in nature.

DAVID: So, has that not been determined? It's by free will?

SUBJECT: Everything will be revealed later.

DAVID: Do we see that some leaders will be able to help with the human condition and show that there's a way within that can get them closer to home or heaven than they are now?

SUBJECT: I don't understand your question.

DAVID: Let's ask this question: There will be followings, but will these followings of the leaders, will these be more of a universal approach to where everyone is one? As opposed to separation practiced by some religions today?

SUBJECT: Not every following will be a movement.

DAVID: Will some try to share what their interpretation is of the words that Jesus spoke 2,000 years ago, among other ascended masters and the religions they built? Will the followings teach how to find heaven and God in their view?

SUBJECT: Even good intentions are flawed.

DAVID: And what flaws in intentions? What could that be?

SUBJECT: We're still only human.

DAVID: So, you see that maybe what starts out as good intentions can unravel into ego?

SUBJECT: Yes.

DAVID: How can one continue to avoid those intentions, by staying always with the light and always have the best intents of others in mind when they make decisions?

SUBJECT: To not elevate one's self.

DAVID: So, you're saying, if one elevates one's self above those he is trying to help, it's bad, is that correct?

SUBJECT: Yes.

DAVID: In other words, if one takes one's wisdom and tries to share it, but maybe at the same time, isn't as accepting as others on their path or journey at that moment, then that's putting themselves above another.

SUBJECT: You have to treat everyone as if they were your brother, the brotherhood of man.

DAVID: So, if I look at everyone as my brother, the brothers I have right now for example, and look at everyone in that particular fashion, not being upset with them for not seeing things the way I see things sometimes, but just having that love in my heart. Will that keep me on the path of good intention?

SUBJECT: Yes.

DAVID: So that should be my primary, foremost thing? Everybody I encounter? Everyone I see, regardless of where they are on their path, or regardless of what they do, is that correct?

SUBJECT: Yes. There can be no judgment.

DAVID: Right. So good or bad, they are all my brothers.

SUBJECT: Yes. One man's problem is the problem of mankind. If unjust, they will answer for the things that they've done.

DAVID: They will answer for what they have done, is that what you are telling me?

SUBJECT: Yes.

DAVID: So, a leader should accept all into his house for understanding regardless of their actions or thoughts, is that correct?

SUBJECT: They will not all be united, though.

DAVID: So, this time that we are in would be called the dawning? How long has the Age of Aquarius been here?

SUBJECT: It started in 2008.

DAVID: Not 1998? Like Edgar Cayce might have thought? Or were we delayed ten years? What do you think?

SUBJECT: It's possible that it was 1998.

Native American Woman

The hypnotic induction that was used in this past life reading was left out as to avoid repetition, as many inductions sound similar. The subject was brought into a deep hypnotic state and recounts a life as a young female Native American Indian in her late teens living in Virginia or West Virginia in the 1700s.

DAVID: I want you just to share with me what you see.

SUBJECT: It's not a town or a city. It's a village.

DAVID: And what kind of structures are in this village?

SUBJECT: They have thatched roofs. They are simply built, and they're not very durable.

DAVID: Do you see people around the village?

SUBJECT: Yes.

DAVID: And what are some of them doing?

SUBJECT: Cooking over fires and sharpening tools.

DAVID: Are they sharpening tools to hunt or...?

SUBJECT: For hunting.

DAVID: Can you describe some outfits they're wearing?

SUBJECT: Looks like leather, but suede, like animal skin.

DAVID: You're floating along in the bubble, just taking it in. You're going to be an observer, and you can step out of your bubble any time you want and move closer toward the scene, whatever you prefer. You are safe, and you can leave your bubble and walk among the people, and they won't be able to see you. Can you do that?

SUBJECT: Yes.

DAVID: And what do you do in the village? Do you know your job or what do you like to do?

SUBJECT: I weave.

DAVID: And what do you weave?

SUBJECT: I weave mats and patches for the roofs.

DAVID: And how old do you think you are in this life, roughly?

SUBJECT: Seventeen or eighteen.

DAVID: So, you can see yourself?

SUBJECT: Yeah.

DAVID: Okay. And what are you wearing?

SUBJECT: A dress that's made out of animal hide, and I have a pouch hanging off my one shoulder.

DAVID: And what do you keep in your pouch?

SUBJECT: Herbs and a knife and tools.

DAVID: What color is your hair? How long is it?

SUBJECT: It's dark... dark... dark brown, almost black. It's long, and I wear it in a braid down my back.

DAVID: Do you know your name?

SUBJECT: Akinowa.

DAVID: Can you say that one more time, please?

SUBJECT: My name was something else like that; it's hard to translate. It was longer than that, but Kinowa was my nickname.

DAVID: Can you see the first letter if it was printed on a piece of paper?

SUBJECT: I don't know how to write it.

DAVID: Because it is in a whole different language, right?

SUBJECT: Well, I don't write.

[I wasn't thinking when I asked the question, as I had not yet approached the subject concerning the time period or tribe she was experiencing in that life to get a better idea of the culture. The first tribe to produce a written language in North America was the Cherokee (called Tsalagi) in 1821. Other tribes adopted written English later or developed their own writing system. It is believed that the Olmecs of Mexico developed a writing system over 3,000 years ago — the oldest known writing in the Americas. The Zapotecs had written by 500 BC (2,500 years ago), and Mayan glyphs appeared in Yucatan, Honduras, Guatemala, and Belize by about 250 BC (2,250 years ago).

All of these were fully developed and complete writing systems, able to record the sounds of their respective languages. Almost all Native Americans throughout the Americas developed a system of pictographs, which are, fundamentally, ways of reminding the viewer about events, people and places, but they are not a proper writing system. Their communication methods are closely related to the primitive prehistoric pictographs of Australian aborigines and the cave art of Europe.]

DAVID: So, you don't know how to write your name, I understand. Well it's a pretty name. Does it mean anything in particular in your tribe or village?

SUBJECT: It means the part of the flower just before it starts to bloom.

DAVID: Nice... now do you have one name or do you have two names or more?

SUBJECT: You have your given name that you are born with, and then some people have a nickname based on their personality or their physical appearance. And you have a name that you take if you marry.

DAVID: Now are you close to marrying, or are you already married?

SUBJECT: I'm married.

DAVID: And what is your husband's name?

SUBJECT: Atchuli.

DAVID: Say that one more time.

SUBJECT: His name is Atchuli.

DAVID: Atchuli, okay, and what does that mean?

SUBJECT: The translation is not exact, but it means someone who is sturdy or someone who is not moved easily. Stubborn, I think is the word.

DAVID: So, a pretty solid, sturdy guy overall.

SUBJECT: Yeah.

DAVID: Do you have children?

SUBJECT: Yeah, we do.

DAVID: How many children?

SUBJECT: I had four.

DAVID: Good. And can you give me a little information on them, their names or how old they are? Boy or girl?

SUBJECT: My oldest is a boy. There's another boy and a baby... baby girl.

DAVID: So, two boys and a baby girl, that's three. Do you have a daughter older than the baby?

SUBJECT: No, I lost a baby. I lost a baby recently.

DAVID: I'm sorry to hear that. So, you have three surviving babies, right?

SUBJECT: Yeah, she's almost a year old.

DAVID: Okay, so sadly, you and Atchuli lost a child not that long ago.

SUBJECT: Yeah.

DAVID: Sorry to hear that, but remember, you are just observing that life as you remember. And what does your husband do for work?

SUBJECT: He's a hunter, and he trades the animal skins and the meats with other men in other villages.

DAVID: And what kind of meat or animals does he get a chance to kill in your area?

SUBJECT: Deer and sometimes bear.

DAVID: Now where is the village located? Is there another village nearby? Give me some idea about that.

SUBJECT: The woods surround a great portion of our village, and on one side of the woods is a stream that widens to a river, and on the other side there's another village.

DAVID: Over by the river?

SUBJECT: Yeah.

DAVID: Do you catch fish, as well, at your village?

SUBJECT: Yes.

DAVID: And what kind of fish? Do you know the names or what they look like, if we had to compare them to today's fish?

SUBJECT: Well they are very big, but the name trout is what they remind me of.

DAVID: And how do you say that in your language?

SUBJECT: It's a silly word.

DAVID: See what it starts with.

SUBJECT: Tia.... Gia.... Giafish [pronounced "ghee-ah-fish"].

DAVID: So, is it almost like "TIA" Fish?

SUBJECT: Gia.

DAVID: Oh Giafish. Do you know how to say bear too? How would you say 'bear' if you were to see it in your mind? Or what would it sound like?

SUBJECT: Sika... Sinka..

DAVID: How about deer? Do you know what the name is in your language for deer?

SUBJECT: An... Ansee... Ansank....

DAVID: Is it a longer word? Just take your time. Let's see if you can hear it in your ears.

SUBJECT: Ansinka.

DAVID: Ansinka, is that close?

SUBJECT: Yeah.

DAVID: And what was your name again?

[Asking the subject names and other pertinent or specific details later in the regression session provides me verification that they are viewing that life with that person's memories. As she was placed in a super-conscious state, the subject literally finds herself back in that life, thus the fast recall when questioned again about certain things.]

SUBJECT: Akinowa.

DAVID: Say that one more time, please.

SUBJECT: Akinowa.

DAVID: And your husband's name?

SUBJECT: Atchuli.

DAVID: Do you remember your children's names, the three that survived? What did you name the baby?

SUBJECT: I don't recall their names.

DAVID: I want you to go deeper and deeper with me. Your mind clears even more, and you see more details of the village and the people working. You might even see yourself working while you are observing. And perhaps you see your husband coming in and out of the thatched wigwam you are living in. And while you look around... do they hunt on foot or horseback?

SUBJECT: They are on foot, but there are horses that other men have brought in from trades.

DAVID: So, they hunt mostly on foot, but there are a few horses that they traded for... Who did they trade with?

SUBJECT: They traded with other men.

DAVID: Okay... for what...?

SUBJECT: For bearskins, for pelts.

DAVID: Now did your husband Atchuli ever kill a bear?

SUBJECT: Yeah, he killed three.

DAVID: Three bears. Did he keep the claws as well as the bearskins?

SUBJECT: He kept one claw from each bear.

DAVID: And did you eat the meat?

SUBJECT: We did.

DAVID: And how did you make it? How does it taste, pretty good?

SUBJECT: It has a heavy taste, but very good for your body.

DAVID: Did you have pots, like a big iron pot, or what did you cook in? Did you wrap it in something or how did you cook bear?

SUBJECT: Mostly over a fire, in an enameled clay pot, not bowl, bigger than that.

DAVID: Now did your village make the bowls?

SUBJECT: No, we traded for them.

DAVID: And they had enameling on the outside or something?

SUBJECT: It was a glaze of some sort.

DAVID: So, they glazed the clay bowls.

SUBJECT: Yes.

DAVID: And that cooked bear pretty well on the fire? The pot didn't get too hot and break?

SUBJECT: Well you cut it up, you don't cook it in one solid piece.

DAVID: How did you get your weapons? Were there any guns in the village or was it just.... did you trade for guns too?

SUBJECT: No, we don't have guns.

DAVID: So, no guns, but do you use rock arrowheads on the end of arrows? Did you have bows and arrows or did you have spears?

SUBJECT: Spears and some people had bows.

DAVID: Now did you make the sharp ends from rocks near you? How did you do that?

SUBJECT: Yeah, from sharp stones.

DAVID: So, you chip them and make them... I presume the tribe would make them that way and tie them on?

SUBJECT: You can grind them against other rocks.

DAVID: So, three bears. Were you real proud of your husband at that point?

SUBJECT: Yes. We were a really good match.

DAVID: And when Atchuli killed the bears, everyone had plenty to eat. Did you share some with other village members?

SUBJECT: The whole village ate.

DAVID: So, the whole village would share in whatever meat came in, right?

SUBJECT: Yes.

DAVID: Was there a lot of rain or did you go through periods that were pretty dry sometimes?

SUBJECT: It would get very cold.

DAVID: It would get very cold?

SUBJECT: Winters were cold.

DAVID: Did you grow anything outside to eat or not?

SUBJECT: No, not really.

DAVID: So, would you eat plants from the woods or did you live on meat mostly? What did you live on? What did you eat?

SUBJECT: There would be meat and berries and nuts, when we could find them, and fish.

DAVID: Fish. Trout. I'm going to ask you again if you could just think in your mind of fish. How did you say trout again or fish in your language?

SUBJECT: [Slight coughing] Gia.

DAVID: Okay, let your throat just relax. Just relax. So, you feel yourself in the village and you were married. And you and your husband... what's his name again?

SUBJECT: Atchuli.

DAVID: Was it a good marriage, you said?

SUBJECT: We were very happy.

DAVID: Well, that's good. He got three bears and had three children. Well as you are relaxing, thinking about that life, and you were seventeen or eighteen then... do you see yourself getting older as the years progress? Do you stay in the same place or do you move somewhere else?

SUBJECT: We stay there and [mumbled].

DAVID: It's okay, you are only observing. What do you see?

SUBJECT: A war. A war with other tribes...with another tribe.

DAVID: Then what happened? And before you go that far into that life to see what happened, I want you to come back with me to the village while you were making your rugs or your mats.

SUBJECT: [coughing].

[I could tell the subject was getting noticeably upset as she was starting to relive the war in her subconscious. I decided it was best to go back to an earlier, happier time. As mentioned in the forward of this book, I have no idea what a deeply regressed subject will share as we proceed through the life they are recounting.]

DAVID: I want you to gently swallow, gently swallow. Now as you are making mats, we'll go back to a better time before the war. You see your children and Atchuli, and you're making mats. How do they describe the country you are in? What do they call it?

SUBJECT: I never heard its name.

DAVID: So, if you had to think of a map right now, and try to picture that place on a map, some country or city, going forward to today, do you see where that might be?

SUBJECT: I think it's in Virginia.

DAVID: Okay.

SUBJECT: West Virginia maybe.

DAVID: So, you see the word Virginia in your mind? Is that right? Or does it just feel like that?

SUBJECT: The name is familiar.

DAVID: And as you think back at seventeen, you begin to see calendars or numbers floating by you in your mind. What year was that roughly? What century?

SUBJECT: 18… 1801. [Cough]

DAVID: So, you think it was around 1801?

SUBJECT: 18… 17… 1781. 1781.

DAVID: So, 1781. And you feel you are in Virginia or West Virginia. When you think about it for a moment, which one do you think it is?

SUBJECT: It's probably southern Virginia.

DAVID: Southern Virginia, maybe in that area?

SUBJECT: Yeah.

DAVID: Somewhere down there. Did you ever.... what color is your skin?

SUBJECT: It is dark.

DAVID: Now did you ever see settlers... people with white skin?

SUBJECT: I heard about them, but I saw one, one time.

DAVID: You saw one, one time?

SUBJECT: There were men that came to trade in our village, and they brought a white man with them.

DAVID: And they were from another village to trade, and brought him with them? Is that correct?

SUBJECT: Yeah.

DAVID: Did he seem like a nice guy or were you a little scared of him? What were your thoughts?

SUBJECT: A woman or oracle from our village told of his coming and said that it was a bad omen.

DAVID: And was the oracle... let's talk about her for a moment. Was she older? What was her background?

SUBJECT: She was older than me, but I wouldn't say she was old.

DAVID: But she was pretty good at seeing things and making prophecy?

SUBJECT: Yes, she had foretold many things.

DAVID: That's interesting. Did she wear her hair like you?

SUBJECT: Yes, but when she was performing ceremonies, she would take it out of her braids.

DAVID: And, did she have dark skin I presume, as well?

SUBJECT: Yes, and very light eyes.

DAVID: Was that something that kind of set her apart from other people in the village?

SUBJECT: They say that it was the mark of her gift.

DAVID: And what color where they? Like light blue or green or amber? What color do you think they were?

SUBJECT: They were almost gray. Like soot.

DAVID: Was she pretty?

SUBJECT: In an odd sort of way, like her face didn't match itself, like there was something out of place.

DAVID: Did she seem... do you think she was from your tribe... who was she born to? Was it anybody in your village or did she just show up? How did that work?

SUBJECT: She was supposed to have been an orphan from a young age. So, she grew up in the village, but she was taken in by a midwife. One of the midwives was the one who noticed her gift.

DAVID: But she came in as an orphan, just kind of stumbled in out of the woods?

SUBJECT: I don't remember where she came from. She was always known to have been orphaned.

DAVID: But she was very good at prophecy?

SUBJECT: She was.

DAVID: And what was her name?

SUBJECT: Shaysha.

DAVID: Was that her only name?

SUBJECT: That was the only name I ever knew her by.

DAVID: Did she seem different from most people in the tribe... not only gifted, but as some special person that came in to help your village?

SUBJECT: She was chosen for that purpose.

DAVID: Now, besides that, did she do anything with medicine or herbs, besides prophecy? Did she have any other gifts?

SUBJECT: She was a healer.

DAVID: So, she could help heal people in the village?

SUBJECT: She was a healer.

DAVID: Did she put her hands on them or just do all sorts of different things?

SUBJECT: She would use different herbs and balms and she would burn things, say prayers.

DAVID: Whom would she pray to?

SUBJECT: To the Great Spirit.

DAVID: So, you knew there was a Great Spirit?

SUBJECT: Well, yes, a Great Spirit.

DAVID: Did he have other spirits to help him? Or did you just know of one?

SUBJECT: The spirit exists in everything, so He is all things everywhere.

DAVID: And that is what your tribe believed, is that correct?

SUBJECT: Yes.

DAVID: Did you ever find yourself praying to Great Spirit to bring something into your life?

SUBJECT: I did the prayers that I was supposed to.

DAVID: Were you angry with Great Spirit when your child died?

SUBJECT: No, I was not angry.

DAVID: You were what?

SUBJECT: I was not angry.

DAVID: Because, why? Because you thought it was supposed to be?

SUBJECT: No, I was just sad.

DAVID: Was it not unusual in your village to lose children to various things? Was it pretty common for every family to maybe lose one or two?

SUBJECT: My final pregnancy had been a difficult one, and the midwife had warned me that I might not be able to have many more children.

DAVID: And did Shaysha work with her, or did they have more than one midwife in the tribe or village?

SUBJECT: There was the midwife, there was usually a girl apprenticing or training with her, but Shaysha was at every birth so she could bless the child.

DAVID: How interesting is that. And as you let your mind take in the moment, and you're getting more and more information, can you tell me what year you think it was again?

SUBJECT: 1781.

DAVID: And you are somewhere... did you say southern Virginia? What are your thoughts on that based on what you've been told or whatever?

SUBJECT: It's southern, but higher altitude, or high elevation.

DAVID: So, you're not in a valley or on flat land?

SUBJECT: No.

DAVID: Can you describe the terrain or the woods? What types of trees are around you in your woods? I know you have more than one species, but what seemed to be the most predominant ones?

SUBJECT: Well, there are many oak trees.

DAVID: Do you live on a mountain range? How does it look when they describe the village?

SUBJECT: There are many hills. It is at the base of a larger hill.

DAVID: So, do you live on the top of the hill or on the side of it?

SUBJECT: Toward the center, near the bottom.

DAVID: The center of the hill but toward the bottom. Am I getting that correct?

SUBJECT: Yeah, yeah.

DAVID: What do they call that river near you? What's the name of that? Do you know? How do they say it in your language?

SUBJECT: Don't know the name.

DAVID: Does the tribe just call it "Great River"? What do they refer to the river as?

SUBJECT: I don't know.

DAVID: So maybe it didn't have a name. Do you remember how they said, "I'm going to the river"? What word they used for river? Or water?

SUBJECT: I can't make the sound.

DAVID: That's all right. Now, go further in time. Everything is going well in the village and all of a sudden, another village... tell me what happened that caused a war. Go ahead.

SUBJECT: The story has been changed, but men who came to trade... well, they traded, but they also stole children. They stole children from our village and sold them.

DAVID: Oh, that's terrible. Was that the village near the river, or was that a different village?

SUBJECT: A village from the other side of the river, but not the one... not the one closest to us.

DAVID: So, they stole children, and whom did they sell them to?

SUBJECT: They sold them to other tribes and then to... not only to other tribes, but to tribes of men that didn't belong here.

DAVID: What color were these men? What color were they?

SUBJECT: I never saw them.

DAVID: So, you never saw the men?

SUBJECT: I never saw what happened to those children. We only heard these stories, and that's what made our village go to war. Children disappeared and that...

DAVID: And it was soon after that or right then?

SUBJECT: Our children would go wandering, and children would go on spirit journeys, and it wasn't uncommon for children to not come home right away, but they were missing. We didn't know where they were.

DAVID: And when they sent men out to the woods, they couldn't find them?

SUBJECT: They didn't find any remains to suggest an animal had attacked or killed them. They didn't find any trace.

DAVID: Were some of the men rumored to not be from Indian tribes or were they all of Indian tribes that came, what do you think?

SUBJECT: The rumor was that they were sold to the white men who were coming on the river.

DAVID: They were coming up the river?

SUBJECT: On the river.

DAVID: They were coming on the river. Were they in some type of boat, or what kind of craft were they in? Were they on horses, or were they on boats? How did they get close?

SUBJECT: I guess they would have come on a boat, but I never saw it.

DAVID: Never saw the boat. How far was the river from your village if you walked to it at an average pace? How long would it take to get there?

SUBJECT: About an hour.

DAVID: So, about an hour walking... roughly?

SUBJECT: Depending on if the weather was good.

DAVID: Now tell me about the weather again. How long was it snowy or cold?

SUBJECT: It felt like it was cold most of the time, but in the summer, when the weather would soften, it would be nice. It would be sunny.

DAVID: And how long would that last? Do you remember roughly, if you had to look at the whole year?

SUBJECT: Three months. Four months. Three months.

DAVID: And then it would be cold again, is that correct?

SUBJECT: It would be cold.

DAVID: So, if you looked at a map, how high do you think you were? 1,000 feet?

SUBJECT: I don't know.

DAVID: But it was high enough that you could see other mountains in the distance?

SUBJECT: Yeah.

DAVID: All right. And did you like your village? Was it pretty?

SUBJECT: Yes, it was the only home I ever knew.

DAVID: So, your village went to war, because the missing children weren't showing up?

SUBJECT: [Emphatically] They stole our children.

DAVID: How many…? Did they steal one of your children?

SUBJECT: They stole my daughter.

DAVID: The baby?

SUBJECT: They stole her.

DAVID: Okay, I want you to just observe and not get emotionally involved. And she was how old again?

SUBJECT: She was a year old.

DAVID: And what was her name? Do you remember?

SUBJECT: Chichka. Something about her...

DAVID: Let's move on...go forward. Looking at your tribe and village. Were you a part of a much bigger tribe? How many villages like yours were parts of the same tribe? Was there a certain tribal name you were known by?

SUBJECT: I don't remember the name of my people.

DAVID: Were there more than just your village, or were there other villages that had the same beliefs as your village?

SUBJECT: I think so, but we were alone. It felt like we were alone where we were. We were isolated.

DAVID: And how many people, say before the children went missing... how many people were in your village roughly? Do you remember? How many wigwams and all of that?

SUBJECT: Maybe over a thousand in tribe.

DAVID: So, it was a pretty nice-sized village, I presume?

SUBJECT: Yes.

DAVID: And how was it broken down? Was it almost an equal number of men and women, or more men, or more women? What did that number look like?

SUBJECT: No, there were a lot of men.

DAVID: More men than women?

SUBJECT: Yeah.

DAVID: Looking at the war, how long did the war last roughly?

SUBJECT: Many months.

DAVID: Did both sides attack each other or did your group go over first? When the children went missing, what happened? Just give me an idea. I know you said the story was changed, but just give me a quick version of what it looked like to you.

SUBJECT: Atchuli and our leaders went to the tribe and we attacked them first. We killed some of their men and wounded others, and then they burned our village.

DAVID: Did Atchuli survive the war? What happened to Atchuli and to you?

SUBJECT: No one survived.

DAVID: That's terrible. So, they burnt the village. They came back and burnt your village. Did they kill everyone in the village?

SUBJECT: They killed everyone.

DAVID: Okay, so now you are just going to observe quietly. What was your name again?

SUBJECT: Akinowa.

DAVID: Don't get wrapped up emotionally. You are just observing — that's all. Just stepping back, don't get involved. Now I want you to tell me, how did you pass away? What happened?

SUBJECT: I was trapped. I burned alive.

DAVID: So, you were trapped inside your wigwam? Is that correct?

SUBJECT: The roof fell in.

DAVID: After they set it on fire?

SUBJECT: Yes.

DAVID: And how fast... how long do you see... let me ask you this, just real lightly, after the roof fell in... I presume it was painful for a while... Was that true?

SUBJECT: Yes.

DAVID: And then how long did it take until you saw yourself standing outside, or standing in the wigwam looking at your body? How long did that take?

SUBJECT: I never experienced that. I remember the pain and then I remember when the pain disappeared, and then I felt nothing.

DAVID: Was anyone there when you felt nothing?

SUBJECT: No, it was like a disintegrating sort of feeling. But there was this feeling of warmth and a peacefulness, like a quiet forest at night.

DAVID: So that's how you felt after you passed away. Is that correct?

SUBJECT: That's when my spirit became a part of everything.

DAVID: So, you felt your spirit... and you said you disintegrated. So, when you passed away and felt this warmth, this relaxation, did you feel your spirit... you said it felt like you separated into everything around you?

SUBJECT: Yes. Like blowing dust.

DAVID: It felt like blowing dust, and you realized you were going back to Mother Earth. And as you are going back to Mother Earth, and felt yourself scattering among everything, did you see little pieces of you in a sense that buried into the trees and the plants? Did you go inside them?

SUBJECT: I don't remember any of that. I just remember being a part of everything.

DAVID: A part of everything. So, after you were a part of everything, and you were in this state of being a part of everything, then what happened?

SUBJECT: That was... that was what I remember.

DAVID: So, you don't remember if there was something more than being a part of everything?

SUBJECT: No.

DAVID: Okay, that's okay. Well, that's good. So, you think it was about 1781, but you don't see yourself coming back again after that war? Do you feel like all of a sudden you became someone else after the war, eventually? And woke up again?

SUBJECT: My spirit became part of everything, so in a way, it was always there and went back.

DAVID: Well let's leave that life now, and let that life drift away as we put that memory to bed. Now you're back in your bubble, flowing back above, past the village, over some mountain ranges. Are you in your bubble now?

SUBJECT: Yes.

DAVID: So, I just want you to float along past that village and that life. Putting that life behind you as you go forward, looking ahead or looking behind you, maybe into an earlier life. Still floating over forest and plains, and mountains and streams, and basically whatever comes into your mind. I want you to float along, exiting that life and moving on past. I want you to keep drifting along in your bubble, putting all of that past behind you.

Moving. Moving, moving forward. And as you move forward, still in your safe, protective bubble, you are just floating along. The sun's rays are coming down to you and golden light is enveloping you in love and Divine love, filling your body again with all of its beautiful light. And as you move along in the bubble, you are going to keep going along, moving along. Just let your mind's eye take in the sights, going slowly along, way past that life you just explored. As I count up from one to five, I want you to awaken more and more with each higher number.

DAVID: Can you do that for me?

SUBJECT: Yes

First Mate O'Brian of the Royal Navy

~

This session was with a female subject in her late-twenties. She went deeply into a hypnotic state and shared a fairly remarkable life.

DAVID: We're going to say a prayer of protection first. We want this to be a reading that is accurate for ------------- to where she finds some information that will help her in this life and maybe discover things she's brought into this life from other past lives. So, we'd like to ask for protection — surrounding ourselves with our guardian angels and archangels. Putting a circle of protection and light around us to where no darkness may enter, only the Christ consciousness and those with love for our highest intent and to protect us during this reading for -------------. I would like to count down from 5-1…

[Hypnosis entry]

[Before any subjects are ever regressed, a prayer of protection is used. The purpose of regression is to help the various subjects in many different ways: gaining a stronger perspective of the immortality of the soul, healing past or current traumas, and learning more about themselves.]

DAVID: Feel your body encased in golden, divine light, seeing yourself resting inside this beautiful bubble of light with your eyes closed. See a beautiful, golden protective layer of bubble energy as it now has encapsulated your body. You feel so safe, so secure, as we count down. Feel relaxed as you're floating inside. Feel yourself just floating along in this beautiful bubble. And you're floating along, just drifting along, floating over a beautiful field, so light and so relaxed. As we count from 5 to 1. And you're feeling so good, just sinking further into the bubble as it's carrying you along very lightly and very nicely on your journey.

Just floating along in this beautiful golden-lit bubble of Divine light, protecting you and just carrying you along on a very mild breeze. Counting down from five to four. Feeling yourself just floating, floating, floating. Hearing my voice, we count from four down to three. Just floating along. So safe and secure as we have our angels around us watching you float along. As we count from three down to two. And as you're floating, all you hear is my voice. Not falling asleep, so relaxed, so relaxed.

As we look to the past at other times, other places, to where you might have lived in another time, a past life. As you're floating along in your bubble, floating along. We're looking for a life or lives that have some impact or meaning on this current life. Your eyes are closed, and your mind's eye is opening up to lives that will benefit you in this life. These are lives that you had in the past, that can help you for your highest good, and that aid your progress going forward in this life. Your bubble floats along — you're just floating along. And you begin to picture some type of a dwelling. And in your mind's eye, you're so relaxed, so relaxed, and when you see something in your mind, I want you to describe it to me.

[Silence]

DAVID: Do you see anything?

SUBJECT: I see a house, a cottage.

DAVID: Describe the cottage. What color is it?

SUBJECT: It's stone with a thatched roof and a chimney on the left side.

DAVID: Are there windows?

SUBJECT: There are two windows.

DAVID: Is it a one-story or a two-story stone house?

SUBJECT: It's two stories.

DAVID: Is there a sidewalk leading up to it or grass?

SUBJECT: It's just a dirt path.

DAVID: And is this where you lived at one time?

SUBJECT: When I was very small.

DAVID: So, when you look at this house, and we're just observers, can we walk up to the front door of the house and open the door?

SUBJECT: You could, but the door is open.

DAVID: Can you walk inside for me, and tell me what you see?

SUBJECT: I see a kitchen on the left, a stove. I see pots. I see cobwebs and dust.

DAVID: Does it look like it hasn't been cleaned in a while? Why would there be cobwebs?

SUBJECT: My mother doesn't clean very often.

DAVID: Now look at the stove. Can you describe that to me?

SUBJECT: It's made out of a potbelly, an iron potbelly stove.

DAVID: Is it being used, or is it just sitting there now?

SUBJECT: It's being used.

DAVID: Do you see yourself in the house? How old are you roughly?

SUBJECT: I'm four.

DAVID: What are you wearing? A dress? Or pants?

SUBJECT: I'm wearing little overall trousers and nothing else.

DAVID: Do you know your name?

SUBJECT: Jacob.

DAVID: Your name is Jacob. And what color is your hair?

SUBJECT: It's a light brown. It's tangled.

DAVID: It's tangled up. Do you have shoes on?

SUBJECT: No.

DAVID: So, you're running around. That sounds like fun. Now, can you see your mother in the kitchen as well or in the house somewhere?

SUBJECT: I see both my parents.

DAVID: What do they look like?

SUBJECT: Angry.

DAVID: [Laughs] They look angry, okay. And do you know what they're angry about?

SUBJECT: They're yelling at each other.

DAVID: So, they're yelling at each other. Do you know what they're yelling about?

SUBJECT: No. No, I don't know. But my dad picked up the kettle off the stove. He hit my mom with it in the head, and she fell on the floor and stopped moving.

DAVID: Now we're just observing this, okay? I know it's upsetting, but we're just observing. Now what do you do when you see this? Are you shocked or surprised?

SUBJECT: I run outside. I run away.

DAVID: So, you ran away. Now, we're just observing, we're just observing. Do you see where you ran too?

SUBJECT: I run into the woods, and I hide in a tree until a search party comes and finds me a day later.

DAVID: And did you stay in the tree all night?

SUBJECT: Yes.

DAVID: Were you nervous or scared?

SUBJECT: Yes.

DAVID: What time of year was this?

SUBJECT: Late summer.

DAVID: So, was the temperature still pretty good at night?

SUBJECT: It was cold, but it was hot the next day.

DAVID: Did you have anything to eat that whole time? Were you getting pretty hungry?

SUBJECT: I didn't eat anything. I didn't have anything to eat.

DAVID: We're just observing. And who came in the search party? Who eventually found you?

SUBJECT: My aunt — my mom's sister — and a constable.

DAVID: So, they came and found you.

SUBJECT: Yeah.

DAVID: And what happened then, once they found you?

SUBJECT: I went with my aunt, and I had to sit in a room with another man and my dad, and they told me that I was going to live with my aunt. I wasn't going to see my dad anymore.

DAVID: And that was pretty upsetting, I presume?

SUBJECT: I was afraid of my dad.

DAVID: So, you went and lived with your aunt. And was she nice to you?

SUBJECT: She was nice.

DAVID: That's good. Now did she live close by the stone house?

SUBJECT: No, she lived over an hour away, two hours.

DAVID: Two hours away. Pretty far away, huh?

SUBJECT: Yeah.

DAVID: And how did you get to your aunt's house?

SUBJECT: I rode in a cart with her.

DAVID: So, you road in a cart with her, it was pulled by…?

SUBJECT: It was horses, like a coach.

DAVID: Did it look kind of like a stagecoach? What did it look like? A cart? Describe it to me.

SUBJECT: It was open, and there was a spot for luggage or heavy things, and we sat there. And there was a driver that took us, and he led the horses.

DAVID: And how many horses were pulling the cart?

SUBJECT: Two.

DAVID: Did they ever tell you what happened to the stone house?

SUBJECT: I never went back there.

DAVID: Was your mother unfortunately killed in that argument?

SUBJECT: I never saw her again. I think my dad killed her and went to jail.

DAVID: Now we're just observing. So, your aunt raised you?

SUBJECT: Yes.

DAVID: And what was your aunt's name?

SUBJECT: Her name was Annie.

DAVID: Annie, that's a nice name. Was she married?

SUBJECT: She was married.

DAVID: Okay, now did you meet her husband too?

SUBJECT: Yeah, my uncle. Uncle had an important job.

DAVID: Do you know what his name was?

SUBJECT: His name was [pause] William.

DAVID: So, it was Aunt Annie and Uncle William?

SUBJECT: Yeah.

DAVID: And your name was Jacob?

SUBJECT: Yes.

DAVID: And what was your last name? Do you remember?

SUBJECT: It was. It was O'Brien. But my aunt's last name was something else. Her last name was Randolph.

DAVID: Okay, so William Randolph and Annie Randolph, is that correct?

SUBJECT: Yeah.

DAVID: Where was the town that they lived? What was the town's name?

SUBJECT: I don't know the name.

DAVID: But it was about an hour or two by horse ride or cart to their house, is that correct?

SUBJECT: Yeah.

DAVID: Were you too young to know the name of your town or where your house was before?

SUBJECT: I think I came from Sheffield.

DAVID: Sheffield. And where was this Sheffield located?

SUBJECT: In the country.

DAVID: And what country is that?

SUBJECT: In England.

DAVID: Sheffield, England. Now in your mind, while you're thinking about this, you have to drive about an hour or two hours away to get to your aunt's house. Can you see your aunt's house in your mind? Your aunt and uncle's house?

SUBJECT: They had more than one house.

DAVID: They had more than one house. You said your uncle was pretty important or had a good job, right?

SUBJECT: Yeah.

DAVID: So, what did he do for a living?

SUBJECT: He worked for the Royal Navy.

DAVID: He worked for the Royal Navy? And what did he do with them? Did you ever know?

SUBJECT: He was a captain, but he retired because of an injury. He had a pension. So, he lived very comfortable.

DAVID: You said he captained. Did he captain ships or did he captain…?

SUBJECT: He was on ships. Very big, big ships.

DAVID: Did he ever share the name of one of those ships with you? Any of the boats he was on? Do you remember any names?

Maybe around the house? A model of one or something? Take your time.

SUBJECT: He had a boat. It was one of his big boats. But he had a boat, a sailboat. And its name was the Dragonfly.

DAVID: So, he named his sailboat the Dragonfly. That's a nice name. And that was his sailboat?

SUBJECT: Yeah, he taught me to sail.

DAVID: Oh, that's neat. Was it fun?

SUBJECT: Yeah, I liked the water.

DAVID: When you look at the water, was it near a lake or was it on the ocean?

SUBJECT: It was the ocean.

DAVID: So, you would go sailing on the ocean with your uncle?

SUBJECT: Yes.

DAVID: And how old were you at that time? Do you remember? When did you first start sailing?

SUBJECT: When I was eight.

DAVID: You became pretty good?

SUBJECT: Not until I was eleven or twelve.

DAVID: And do you remember how long this sailboat was roughly? What would you guess?

SUBJECT: It was over thirty feet long.

DAVID: When you look at the water and the sailboat, where was the sailboat kept?

SUBJECT: We had a dock at the house. Not the cottage, the cove. There was a house.

DAVID: What was this house?

SUBJECT: That was their beachfront house. Their house was on the beach.

DAVID: Now do you remember where their beachfront house was located?

SUBJECT: In something Cove. Cove Road.

DAVID: So, was that the name of the road they lived on, or was that the name of the cove?

SUBJECT: Cove Road.

DAVID: Now, if you were near Sheffield, where you were originally as a young child, and now you're about eleven or so years old, let's go forward a few more years. Do you see yourself at sixteen or eighteen?

SUBJECT: I see myself at eighteen.

DAVID: And were you still sailing then? What were you doing at that age?

SUBJECT: I worked for the Royal Navy. I worked on the ships.

DAVID: Wow. So, you got a job with the Royal Navy too? And what was your last name again?

SUBJECT: O'Brien.

DAVID: Now when you were eighteen, what year did you get that job?

SUBJECT: It was 1867.

DAVID: So, you're pretty sure it was 1867, is that correct?

SUBJECT: Yes, it was 1867.

DAVID: Now when you look back at 1867, that was when you were eighteen, right?

SUBJECT: Yeah.

DAVID: So, were you born in 1851 maybe or do you not know? What year were you born?

SUBJECT: I was born in 1850.

DAVID: And do you see the month of your birth? What was your birthday? Do you see the month and the day?

SUBJECT: March 28, 1850

DAVID: So, March 28, 1850, is that correct?

SUBJECT: March 28th.

DAVID: And do you have a middle name? Do you remember?

SUBJECT: It was my father's name.

DAVID: So, your middle name was your father's name, is that correct?

SUBJECT: Yeah.

DAVID: And what was your father's name? I don't remember asking you that.

SUBJECT: His name was Samuel.

DAVID: Samuel. So, what was your full name again?

SUBJECT: Jacob Samuel O'Brien.

DAVID: So, you worked for the Royal Navy. What were some of the names of the ships you worked on? Do you remember?

SUBJECT: They all had names of women. They were named after women.

DAVID: Out of all the ships named after women that you worked on, what was your favorite one?

SUBJECT: It was a big ship. It was expensive to crew because it was large, because the masts were tall.

DAVID: So how many masts did that ship have? Do you remember?

SUBJECT: Almost two-dozen.

DAVID: Two-dozen masts?

SUBJECT: Sails.

DAVID: Two-dozen sails, Okay. So, when we look at the masts. How many big masts were on that ship? Do you remember?

SUBJECT: There were four.

DAVID: There were four masts, okay. And where did that ship sail?

SUBJECT: The Indian Ocean.

DAVID: So, you went to the Indian Ocean. Did it go to any other countries?

SUBJECT: We were in tropical islands.

DAVID: So, you were on the Indian Ocean, and you were sailing to tropical islands. Can you give me the name of some of those islands?

SUBJECT: They didn't have names.

DAVID: They didn't have names at the time? They were just unnamed, unexplored islands? Do you remember?

SUBJECT: They were remote, and they did not have very many people living on them.

DAVID: So, you would sail. Would you sail from England and then go to the Indian Ocean? How long were you gone?

SUBJECT: Two, sometimes three years.

DAVID: Two to three years? Does that sound about right?

SUBJECT: I went on long expeditions because of the nature of my position with the navy. I was responsible for repairs, and I also managed the log. I had to keep journals.

DAVID: So, you kept records of your journeys, is that correct?

SUBJECT: I kept records.

DAVID: Was this one of the ships that you were on the most or for the longest period?

SUBJECT: Yeah.

DAVID: And how many crewmembers would go out and sail with you on these long voyages?

SUBJECT: About… With crew hands and the Captain, it would have been about thirty men.

DAVID: Thirty men, Okay. And what was your position called? Did you have a title or a position? What was your position?

SUBJECT: I didn't have a title. I was sort of given the job because of my uncle's influence.

DAVID: What was your captain's name that was on that ship the most? What was his name?

SUBJECT: His name was… [pause]

DAVID: What did it start with?

SUBJECT: His name was James Chesterfield.

DAVID: That was his name? Was he a good captain?

SUBJECT: He was. He was a stingy captain, but he was intelligent. He knew his way around the ocean.

DAVID: How was he stingy? Did he stop paying well? Was the food bad? How was he stingy?

SUBJECT: He would always try to cut corners on payments. If he said he was paying you a certain amount, it was almost guaranteed that it would be maybe half that when you got home.

DAVID: Well, that is stingy. Give me an idea. Were you paid by the voyage or the week? How did they pay you?

SUBJECT: It would depend on the ship and the captain, and it would depend on the voyage.

DAVID: Let's say you're on the ship and you're going to these remote islands for two or three years. When you came back from one of those voyages, what kind of money did you make?

SUBJECT: The money could be good if we accomplished what we were meant to accomplish, which might have meant taking natural resources from the islands that we found on the islands. Other times we went ashore to bring back certain plants, bringing back certain types of stone or a certain spice. Some voyages were more cut and dry, and some we made more money than we anticipated.

DAVID: And then you would go back to England, I presume, with some of these new treasures or new resources?

SUBJECT: We had people who commissioned us to take them to certain islands so that they could study plants and tropical species.

DAVID: Do you remember who the queen was at this time? Was there a king or queen? Who was running England?

SUBJECT: Victoria.

DAVID: Okay, so there was a Queen Victoria. Was she married, did she have a husband or not?

SUBJECT: She did not. He had died.

DAVID: Let's go forward some years. Do you see yourself in your twenties or thirties?

SUBJECT: Yes.

DAVID: And what are you doing?

SUBJECT: I was part of a voyage to southern — to the southern points of land in the Atlantic Ocean. We were looking for gold.

DAVID: Now when you say, "southern points," where would that be? Is there a name?

SUBJECT: We wound up somewhere in Argentina.

DAVID: And did you find gold?

SUBJECT: We did, but the people that lived in this place when we came to it were not familiar to our customs. We were not familiar to theirs. And the expedition did not go well.

DAVID: So how old were you then? Roughly?

SUBJECT: Thirty-three.

DAVID: Thirty-three-years-old. And you see yourself now. How much bigger are you now? What do you look like now?

SUBJECT: I'm tall. I have very broad shoulders. I have shoulder-length hair that I keep tied back. I have a beard. My hair is a sort of dark blond-light brown color. I look like — I look like my father.

DAVID: And how tall do you think you were?

SUBJECT: I'm about six foot.

DAVID: Well, it sounds like you're a pretty good sailor at this time, right?

SUBJECT: I was very skilled.

DAVID: And did you have a different job at this time?

SUBJECT: I was promoted. I was serving as first mate.

DAVID: First mate. That's a nice job. And who was the captain on this expedition? Do you remember his name?

SUBJECT: Fredericks. Captain Fredericks. I don't remember his first name.

DAVID: Let's go forward some years — what year is it now, roughly?

SUBJECT: 1888.

DAVID: So, you think it was 1888? How old were you?

SUBJECT: I'm 38. I'm 38.

DAVID: What year were you born again? Do you remember?

SUBJECT: 1850. March 28, 1850.

DAVID: March 28, 1850. Okay.

SUBJECT: I was 38-years-old when I died.

DAVID: What year was that?

SUBJECT: It was in 1888. May the 12th.

DAVID: You died on May the 12th. And what did you — we're just observing. You're 38-years-old, and it was May 12th, 1888, and do you remember what you died from?

SUBJECT: There was a member of our crew who had been stealing and when I discovered his thievery, we fought. He stabbed me and pushed me overboard.

DAVID: Now we're just observing. What was his name? Do you remember? I want you to just observe. I just want you to step back and observe. You're not getting involved emotionally. Can you do that for me?

SUBJECT: Yes.

DAVID: All we're doing is observing, and we'll just look at all the facts, but we're not getting involved emotionally, right?

SUBJECT: Okay.

DAVID: Don't get involved emotionally; we're just looking at that life. That life is not here anymore. Do you remember the individual's name?

SUBJECT: His name was John Waters.

DAVID: And where were you pushed overboard? Do you remember if you were at sea or where were you?

SUBJECT: We had made port, but we were on the boat.

DAVID: Now I want you to just observe. Now where did he stab you? Do you remember?

SUBJECT: [Sharp inhale] He stabbed me in the lower abdomen.

DAVID: Now we're just going to observe, is that okay?

SUBJECT: Yes.

DAVID: Here's how we're going to get through this. I am here with you, and you're in a golden bubble of light protection, okay?

So, we're just looking at this. We're not getting involved emotionally. Can you do that?

SUBJECT: Yes.

DAVID: So, you were pushed overboard. Then what happened?

SUBJECT: I —

DAVID: Don't tell me emotional things, just facts. Just think and observe.

SUBJECT: I fell overboard, and I couldn't swim because of where I had been stabbed. I drowned.

DAVID: Now, just observe. We're just observing together, the two of us, no one else. And we're just looking at that life, and you're not getting emotionally involved. We're just looking at the life. And after you drowned, then what happened?

SUBJECT: It felt like a dream. My body was stuck under the water, and I thought that I saw my mother. She pulled me loose and took me out of the water with her.

DAVID: And you came up through the water?

SUBJECT: Yes. Not my physical body though. That stayed.

DAVID: So, you felt like it was a dream. And you saw your mother, your mother that passed when you were only four years old. Was she underwater and helped to pull you out of your body?

SUBJECT: Yes.

DAVID: So, you came out with your mother. Was she holding your hand?

SUBJECT: She was.

[Our deceased family members, friends and others who are departed are aware of our journey here through our entire lives. Jacob's mother had not seen her son physically since she was murdered decades earlier, but she was there instantaneously at his death to help him move into the light. Souls in the spirit world have their own things that they work on and do, but still like to follow the progress of their children or loved ones that are experiencing their earthly lives. This should provide the reader comfort, knowing that our departed loved ones, though on a different dimensional plane, are well aware of our journey through life.]

DAVID: And then what happened? Where did you go?

SUBJECT: And then I wasn't there anymore. I don't know where I went.

DAVID: So, your mother pulled your hand. Let's think about that for a moment. She helped you out of the body that had drowned, right?

SUBJECT: Yes.

DAVID: She helped you come all the way up, and did you both come out of the water together or where were you?

SUBJECT: She helped me. She helped me leave.

DAVID: And when she helped you leave, then what did you see in your mind?

SUBJECT: I just saw the horizon on the water.

DAVID: Oh, was that a pretty sight?

SUBJECT: It was blinding. The light was so bright.

DAVID: So, you saw the horizon. And the light was so bright. Now describe the light to me, besides it being blinding. Did you hear music or feel anything?

SUBJECT: No, I just felt very calm, like the moment in the morning after the sun rises before anything else has really woken up.

DAVID: So, you felt relaxed and calm right?

SUBJECT: Yes, I just felt very calm.

DAVID: Where did you go from there after you saw the light? I want you to just stop and think about it for a moment.

SUBJECT: I didn't go anywhere. I stayed there in the light.

DAVID: Stayed right in the light. Was your mother still with you?

SUBJECT: I don't know. I don't know.

DAVID: Did anyone come to see you in the light?

SUBJECT: I wasn't alone, but I didn't feel the specific identities of other people.

DAVID: Did you see yourself in that light?

SUBJECT: There wasn't really anything to see. I just was.

DAVID: Okay, you, "just was." You felt like there were other souls around you, but there were no particular identities? Were you all just sort of together?

SUBJECT: It was the collective energy or consciousness or something cohesive but not singled out.

DAVID: And what did that feel like then? Did it feel like you were part of something bigger? What did it feel like?

SUBJECT: The truest sense of home, of belonging in something or to something and returning to it.

DAVID: Was it warm or just… did you feel… what kind of emotions did you feel there?

SUBJECT: Just peace.

DAVID: Just peace. Do you know how long you were there?

SUBJECT: I don't know if there was a time that I left. It felt like I was there for a minute but maybe I was there for years.

DAVID: So, it was hard to tell time, wasn't it? Not like here. Is that right?

SUBJECT: There was not a sense of time, no sense of anything.

DAVID: Just part of something, peaceful, but not… did you feel like you had retained some of your personality traits from your earlier life as Jacob?

SUBJECT: I don't remember. I suppose.

DAVID: Now as we look at that life, why was it important for you to know about that life now?

SUBJECT: The way that I grew up as a child in that life — I was disadvantaged, and I came from very tormented people and

I was able to have a different life than what I would have been given because of my aunt, and I was able to work hard enough to achieve things beyond what I previously conceived for myself.

DAVID: So that was a pretty good life as far as growing and becoming somebody you were proud to be, is that right?

SUBJECT: Yes, my career was very important to me, and my aunt was very proud.

DAVID: Well, it sounds like a wonderful life. And the Royal Navy sounds very, very cool too. Now, we drift away, as we leave that life now. Now we drift away from that life as Jacob and just go on, just back in the bubble again, just floating along. Just floating away from that life.

Orphan Twins

It is not unusual for souls entwined in one life to meet again in another life and even cross paths multiple times in many different lives. Very interesting details unfold around this reunion where a female subject in her late-twenties is regressed and recounts a life where her father in her current life was her twin in another life over 100 years ago.

DAVID: [End of Hypnotic Induction] You're just drifting along in the bubble, drifting along, very slowly on the winds. Do you see anything in your mind's eye that would help you from this past life in your current life?

SUBJECT: My dad was [pause] my family before. My dad in my life now used to be my twin.

DAVID: Your dad now used to be your twin. Your dad in this life was your twin in the life we're exploring now?

SUBJECT: Yeah.

DAVID: And where was this life?

SUBJECT: It was in the early 1900s — 1910, 1911. We were born in a city, and we had an older brother, and our parents were killed in an accident. We were orphaned.

DAVID: And where was this located?

SUBJECT: It was in a city in Massachusetts.

DAVID: And do you know your name and your twin's name?

SUBJECT: My name was Elliot. And his name… his name was Peter.

DAVID: And it was about 1910 or 1911. Was that when you were born? How old were you then?

SUBJECT: We were six.

DAVID: Six. So, you were born around 1903 or '04?

SUBJECT: We were born in 1903.

DAVID: What day and month was that? Do you remember?

SUBJECT: August the first.

DAVID: And what town were you born in?

SUBJECT: We were born in a city near Boston.

DAVID: A city near Boston. It was outside of Boston?

SUBJECT: It was maybe an hour away.

DAVID: So, it was 1903. What month and date again?

SUBJECT: August first.

DAVID: And what was your last name?

SUBJECT: Our last name was Brooks.

DAVID: Brooks. And we're just observing this. So, let's go forward in time. Let's go to when you're about ten years old. Are you and your twin still together?

SUBJECT: We're still together.

DAVID: Are you still living in the same area? Where are you? Where are you now?

SUBJECT: We're living in a boys' school for children that are delinquent or wards of the state. We were in an orphanage when we were younger but then our brother was adopted — we were not taken with him — and we never found another home.

DAVID: You never found a home? So, how long did you stay at the orphanage?

SUBJECT: Only a few years. We ran away.

DAVID: So, you and your twin ran away?

SUBJECT: [Sounding proud] Yeah, it was my idea.

DAVID: And where did you run to?

SUBJECT: We just left. We didn't wanna…

DAVID: So, you just left the boys school? Where did you travel to after that?

SUBJECT: We just lived on the street. We did what we could.

DAVID: And how old were you when you and your twin lived on the street?

SUBJECT: About twelve.

DAVID: Let's go forward to when you're about sixteen. Do you see yourself then?

SUBJECT: I do.

DAVID: What are you doing now?

SUBJECT: [Concerned, voice quavering] I don't see Peter.

DAVID: You don't see Peter. Okay. Well let's go back to about thirteen or fourteen. How old were you the last time you saw Peter?

SUBJECT: Fourteen, turning fifteen.

DAVID: Fourteen turning fifteen. What happened to Peter? We're just observing.

SUBJECT: [Voice trembling] He got sick. He got some sort of cough. He had a fever and we took him to the hospital, but they couldn't help him. And I couldn't pay them, and he … he died. He died.

[The subject was understandably upset upon learning of her twin Peter's death. I decided to shift away from the scene and began to ask recall questions to verify details the subject provided earlier. Normally, this approach brings the client to a more detached state from the recently witnessed trauma and reinforces that we are just observing and not getting emotionally involved. This method is referenced in several past life regressions that also led to tragic lives in this book.]

DAVID: We're not going to get involved, okay? We're just going to observe. Did you ever find out what kind of cough it was, or what made Peter sick? Did they ever know what they thought it was?

SUBJECT: It was some kind of virus.

DAVID: And were you still in Massachusetts at that time?

SUBJECT: We were in Boston then.

DAVID: So, you were living in Boston. And what was your last name again?

SUBJECT: Brooks. My name was Elliot Brooks.

DAVID: And your brother was Peter Brooks. We're not getting involved. When Peter passed, do you remember what day that was?

SUBJECT: It was right after our birthday.

DAVID: So, it was right after your birthday.

SUBJECT: It was August 19th.

DAVID: And what year was that? Do you see the year?

SUBJECT: It was 1917.

DAVID: And it was in Boston. Well, let's go forward with your life as Elliot. Now…let's not get emotionally involved. And what do you see with Elliot in his later years? What do you see?

SUBJECT: I'm not a nice person. I steal, I lie, and I drink too much. And I can't keep a job, because I drink too much. And I end up in jail. And then after… after I get out of jail, I drink too much one night after being let out, and I don't wake up the next day. I don't wake up. I was sixteen-seventeen.

DAVID: Years old?

SUBJECT: I was maybe just turned seventeen. I didn't live very long.

DAVID: So, you just turned seventeen. We're not getting emotionally involved. And you think you passed away because you drank too much that night or something?

SUBJECT: I threw up. I choked or something.

DAVID: We're only observing. And you're still in Boston, is that correct?

SUBJECT: Yeah.

DAVID: You got sick and you threw up, and suffocated on your throw-up, is that correct?

SUBJECT: Yes.

DAVID: And then what happened when you died?

SUBJECT: I stayed. I sort of hung around the city. I didn't leave. I didn't know that I could.

DAVID: You stayed around the city, because you didn't know that you could actually leave. Is that correct?

SUBJECT: Yes.

DAVID: And where did you go as a spirit? Could you walk through walls now? Tell me about that.

SUBJECT: I could climb onto a roof and sit on a roof. I could move down through the ceiling and go into a house.

DAVID: And when you went into other houses, were people there?

SUBJECT: I could see them, but I couldn't hear them. It was like listening to sounds underwater.

DAVID: Did they ever sense your presence? Did any animals, like a cat or a dog, sense you? Did they ever notice you? Did anyone ever sense that you were around even though they couldn't see you?

SUBJECT: Well, I made animals very nervous.

DAVID: And they could kind of sense you?

SUBJECT: Yeah, horses or dogs or cows. Yeah, they didn't like it.

DAVID: Oh, that's interesting. And how long did you do that for, checking out other houses and things?

SUBJECT: I don't know… until I left the city, and… I didn't have to stay there. I found a way to leave.

[It's an interesting answer by subject that "he didn't know how long" he remained as a spirit running around Boston. Time in the spirit world only exists as "markers" for events. Our "markers," like birthdays and marriages, have hours, days, weeks, and years in between them. The spirit world does not have days, weeks, or years between their events. The marker was leaving the city of Boston, but Elliot couldn't quantify how long that time actually was. Dates and ages that he shares in remarkable detail are another example of markers on his timeline, which he can recall with great clarity.]

DAVID: That's very interesting. How did you find a way to leave?

SUBJECT: I spent a lot of time watching people and people that I had known and people that I didn't know, and I watched enough life happen the way that mine had happened, and I watched the way that it ended, the way that mine had ended. And I went looking for Peter. I wanted to know if he was there or if he had left or if I could find him. And one day Peter found me. And he told me that I didn't have to stay there if I didn't want to, that I could go with him.

DAVID: And where did you go?

SUBJECT: To another place.

DAVID: Did he help you get there?

SUBJECT: Well, yeah.

DAVID: So how did he help you get there? Did he hold your hand and say, "We're going"? How did he do it?

SUBJECT: He just hugged me.

DAVID: And how did he find you? Do you remember? Was he a spirit hanging out in Boston too? How did he find you?

SUBJECT: He told me that he had been looking for me.

DAVID: Isn't that something? So as a spirit, you could go around and see things, and go through walls and jump on roofs. As a spirit, did you see a lot of other spirits also hanging around?

SUBJECT: Certain places, yeah.

DAVID: So certain places they would hang out, is that correct?

SUBJECT: Yes.

DAVID: And they could see others that were in spirit form, but people who were alive couldn't see them, is that correct?

SUBJECT: Sometimes you could see them. Sometimes they looked like mist with more of a solid shape. Some of them looked just like people — you almost couldn't tell the difference.

DAVID: Between a spirit and someone living?

SUBJECT: Yes.

DAVID: So, Peter was walking around looking for you as you were looking for him?

SUBJECT: Yeah.

DAVID: So, he found you one day walking or floating around, and you ran into him, or how did that work?

SUBJECT: He found me.

DAVID: So, he kind of zoned in and found you, is that correct?

[Unfortunately, the subject couldn't describe how Peter actually "zoned in" to find Elliot.]

SUBJECT: Yeah, he said he was looking for me.

DAVID: So, when he found you and you both left, describe where you went.

SUBJECT: We just went home. We went to a home.

DAVID: You went to a home. Was it up in the light? Was it in the light, or where was it?

SUBJECT: It reminded me of a postcard that I saw. It had a farm picture with a big house and a windmill, and there were sheep, and that's like the place that we went.

DAVID: It sounds pretty nice.

SUBJECT: It was nice.

DAVID: And did you both live there?

SUBJECT: Yeah, we stayed there for a long time.

DAVID: Now were other people with you, or was it just the two of you?

SUBJECT: No, there were a lot of people.

DAVID: And was that like heaven?

SUBJECT If you want to call it that.

DAVID: Was it like earth in a sense? It was a nice, beautiful farm with a windmill and sheep? Were there cows?

SUBJECT: No, there were some things that were like earth, but... it's all the same.

DAVID: Well it sounds really nice, and you stayed there for quite some time?

SUBJECT: Yup. Yeah, we stayed there.

DAVID: And you felt calm? Peaceful there?

SUBJECT: Yeah, that was the only place where we ever really felt at home.

DAVID: Well, let me ask you this then: Why is it important for you to know the life we're reviewing, in this life?

SUBJECT: My dad now, who was Peter, is someone who I feel connected to in a way that I don't know what I'll do when I lose him. But we've found each other before, and even when he dies, even though I won't be ready, I know that we'll find each other again.

DAVID: Definitely. No doubt. And that's good to know, isn't it? That you'll never be apart forever, even though you'll be apart temporarily at times from departed loved ones. Isn't that right?

SUBJECT: Yeah, he'll find me again. I'll find him.

DAVID: Good. Well, let's leave that life now, knowing the good information you've been given, and that you know you'll find your loved ones again, right? Is that how you feel?

SUBJECT: Yeah.

The Tragically Short Life of Laura

The client was guided into a deep hypnotic induction and brought into a super-conscious state where they were capable of exploring a past-life and what they experienced afterward. I was quite taken back by whom they met on the other side and the heavenly "connections" they experienced.

DAVID: [Hypnotic Induction ends] I want you to visualize another life, maybe another home, another place. And when you see it come to you, I want you to tell me what you see, as you float along. Take your time. Let it develop for you. And tell me what you see.

SUBJECT: [Pause] I see two people arguing.

DAVID: And what are they arguing about?

SUBJECT: Menial things. [Pause] It seems like they have a very caustic relationship.

DAVID: Are these two people married?

SUBJECT: Yes.

DAVID: As you're observing this life, and these two people arguing, is one of the people you?

SUBJECT: No, they're my parents.

DAVID: They're your parents, okay. As we sit back and observe, not getting emotionally attached, just watching these two people. Where are they arguing?

SUBJECT: In a kitchen.

DAVID: Can you describe the kitchen to me? What does it look like?

SUBJECT: It has oak cabinets and white countertops, and it's open. It's not very big. There's a sink by a window.

DAVID: Does it look like a newer kitchen or an older kitchen?

SUBJECT: It's not new, but it's not old.

DAVID: Do you remember your mother's name?

SUBJECT: Tracey.

DAVID: What was your dad's name?

SUBJECT: Andrew.

DAVID: So, as you see your parents, how old do you think they are? As they're arguing in the kitchen, how old do they look?

SUBJECT: Maybe in their forties, late thirties. They look tired; it makes them look older than they are.

DAVID: And why are you observing these parents arguing?

SUBJECT: Because I'm too small to be able to leave.

DAVID: And do you see yourself as a boy or a girl?

SUBJECT: I'm a girl.

DAVID: As you just observe, and we're in the kitchen together, what do you look like? Can you describe yourself?

SUBJECT: I'm five, and I have curly blond hair. And my mom puts it in pigtails.

DAVID: Are you wearing a dress or pants or jeans or what?

SUBJECT: I'm wearing a dress.

DAVID: Do you want to describe it to us?

SUBJECT: It has polka dots on it. [Pause] Red-polka-dots.

DAVID: And is it sad for you to see them argue?

SUBJECT: They argue all the time.

DAVID: Do they both work?

SUBJECT: No. My mom says my dad doesn't work, he just drinks.

DAVID: And are you Caucasian? What nationality are you?

SUBJECT: My parents are white.

DAVID: Now, do you see yourself as white?

SUBJECT: Yeah, I'm really pale.

DAVID: And what was your name?

SUBJECT: [Pause] [Confused mumbling]

DAVID: Does it start with any particular letters, do you think? [Pause, waiting] Why don't we try this: Let's go into your bedroom. Go to the bedroom for me. Can you go to your room?

SUBJECT: Okay.

DAVID: What does your room look like? How big is it?

SUBJECT: My room is… is big for me.

DAVID: Let's go outside now in your yard and look at the house. As you go out through the door, just turn around and look. You're floating along in the bubble, just observing. What does your house look like?

SUBJECT: My house is white with blue shutters, and it has a front porch, and the roof hangs over the porch with a window upstairs. And there's a tree at the end of my driveway.

DAVID: Can we look at your mailbox? Let's float over toward that. What number is on your mailbox? Can you see the number?

SUBJECT: [Immediately] 482.

DAVID: 482?

SUBJECT: Yeah.

DAVID: Now if we walk down the street together, you are just observing in the bubble, you're going along, and I'm going with you. Let's go to the corner of your street. Can we do that together?

SUBJECT: Yeah.

DAVID: Let's float up next to the road sign. Tell me the name of the street.

SUBJECT: Cedar Street.

DAVID: So, it looks like Cedar Street to you?

SUBJECT: [Hesitant] Yeah. [More certain] Yeah.

DAVID: Is there another street that crosses your street?

SUBJECT: It's something "hollow" drive. Something-Hollow Drive.

DAVID: Good. Now let's think really hard together. Let's go back to your house. Okay?

SUBJECT: Okay.

DAVID: So, let's drift back down to your house. Let's stand in the front yard, maybe by the tree. Do you have a garage? Is it attached or not attached?

SUBJECT: We have a garage. It's not attached.

DAVID: Does it sit back farther from the house?

SUBJECT: Yeah, but not really far. It's only a couple feet.

DAVID: And how long have you lived in this house?

SUBJECT: As long as I can remember.

DAVID: So, you think maybe you came home from the hospital, and you lived in that house?

SUBJECT: Yeah.

DAVID: Now do you see your name yet? Is there anything in your room that might tell us your name? Maybe something on a wall, a bulletin board, or something?

SUBJECT: [Pause] I think my name is Laura.

DAVID: Now let's walk back out into the kitchen together. Let's just observe and not get involved emotionally with your parents arguing. I want you to look around the kitchen, maybe the living room, or perhaps there's a desk in the house. I want you to walk up to where there are some envelopes, and I want you to look down at the envelopes. Take your time. Tell me what last name is on those envelopes? Can you do that?

SUBJECT: It's Guffy.

DAVID: Like G-U-F-F-Y?

SUBJECT: Yeah.

DAVID: And as you're looking at that envelope, what are the initials of that state?

SUBJECT: It starts with an M.

DAVID: Now what letter is that second letter? Is it a vowel or a consonant? What letter does it look like?

SUBJECT: M-I.

DAVID: Like an 'I'?

SUBJECT: It's MI.

DAVID: Very good. Now let's just sit back and look around and just observe. Describe the living room or where everyone hangs out to me. Describe that to me.

SUBJECT: The walls are white. There's a fireplace and a couch and two armchairs and a rocking chair by one window.

DAVID: Do you ever sit in the rocker? Do you see yourself rocking?

SUBJECT: No, my mom does.

DAVID: Now let's gently go back to that envelope that you saw.

SUBJECT: Okay.

DAVID: What was the name of the town in front of that MI? What was the name of the town?

SUBJECT: I don't know.

DAVID: Okay, do you see the letter it might start with? Take your time. Just kind of look down with your mind's eye, take your time, and tell me what letters the town starts with.

SUBJECT: It starts with C-O-N.

DAVID: Okay, that's good. Is it two syllables? Maybe, two or three or just one?

SUBJECT: It's a long word.

DAVID: Okay, so it starts with C-O-N. Now just take your time, no rush, and tell me the next two when you get the next two after C-O-N. Just take your time.

SUBJECT: [Pause] S-T

DAVID: You're just looking at the envelope with me — I'm looking at it with you — do you see C-O-N-S-T, is that correct?

SUBJECT: Yes.

DAVID: Now, let's just be relaxed, and kind of hover over the envelope. And as the other letters become more apparent to you…

SUBJECT: [Sharp inhale]

DAVID: …You can tell me, okay? What do you see after that 'T'?

SUBJECT: I shouldn't be going through grownup things.

[A subject in a deep, super-conscious state is living that past life fully. In this case, it is as a very young Laura, who was probably scolded in the past for going through her parent's things.]

DAVID: I'm sorry, say that again.

SUBJECT: I don't want to get yelled at.

DAVID: No one here is going to yell at you. It's just you and me all alone; you're protected, okay? So, you're not going to get yelled at, I promise you. I am here with you, and they are just arguing. They're not aware of us. All we're doing is observing. We're not touching the envelopes or their things, so it's okay. You won't get in trouble, I promise. And once we get the name we'll go on somewhere else, okay? That's a promise.

SUBJECT: I don't want to get yelled at.

DAVID: You won't. Now, I want you to go forward if you can with me. Can we do that together?

SUBJECT: Okay.

DAVID: Let's not worry about the envelope now. If we went outside though, do you think there were maybe letters in the mailbox, or had the mail already been brought in today?

SUBJECT: It's sitting on the desk.

DAVID: So, as we go forward, what were some of the most memorable times in this life as Laura? What do you see? What pops into your mind?

SUBJECT: I didn't have a long life.

DAVID: You didn't have a long life?

SUBJECT: No.

DAVID: Can we talk about that? You're just observing. Can you do that with me?

SUBJECT: Yes.

DAVID: You're very relaxed. We're just observing. Can you do this without getting emotional?

SUBJECT: Yes.

DAVID: I'm going to help you through this, okay? I'm here with you. All we're doing is observing the life of Laura. We're not getting involved. It's just like reading a book. We're just looking at the life, not getting emotionally involved. Just observing from a distance. Can we do that?

SUBJECT: Okay.

DAVID: It's just you and me. Okay?

SUBJECT: Okay.

DAVID: Does that make you feel a little better?

SUBJECT: Yeah.

DAVID: Nothing is going to touch us. Nothing is going to hurt us. God is on our side. Do you know who God is?

SUBJECT: Yes.

DAVID: Good, I want you to know He's with us. So, you have nothing to be afraid of. Okay, Laura?

SUBJECT: Okay.

[Though I was unaware at this time where this regression was going, since the subject shared that her life as Laura was short, I intuitively felt it was important to assure her that nothing could happen to her. As mentioned, a prayer of protection is said before each reading, and often this provides comfort for the client. This sets the stage for the hypnotic induction. As this family lived up in the Michigan area and were Caucasian, I took a stab that their beliefs were probably geared around the Bible and some branch of Christianity.]

DAVID: It's just you, God and me together. And Jesus. Is that okay?

SUBJECT: Yes.

DAVID: And you believe in Jesus, right?

SUBJECT: Yes.

DAVID: Okay, good. So, do you feel a little safer now with me and surrounded by the love and light of God and Jesus?

SUBJECT: Yes.

DAVID: And the angels, right? So, all we're doing is just sitting down together, just watching something like a film of Laura. But we're watching away at a distance, like watching a movie, right?

SUBJECT: [Whispered] Okay.

DAVID: We're not going to get involved, and we'll just talk about it. We don't have to get involved. We're just observing and not being emotional, all right?

SUBJECT: Okay.

DAVID: Now what did — How long did you see the life of Laura? How old was she? [Pause, waiting] Do you remember?

SUBJECT: She was… she was fifteen.

DAVID: Now we're not getting emotionally involved ------------. Anything you're holding, you're going to release -------------, anything bad or tragic with this life. We're going to just observe it, and let it go, so that you can move forward and heal as ----------, okay? Does that sound good?

SUBJECT: Okay.

DAVID: So, what we're going to do is just gently observe it, and anything you've locked inside that is negative or hurtful, or makes you feel pain from the life as Laura, you're going to learn from that life and release. But you're not going to let the pain and trauma from that life hold you back in this life. Okay?

SUBJECT: Yeah. [Breathes deeply].

DAVID: Okay, I'm here right now, holding your hand. I want you to just relax. Don't think about it, and tell me when you're ready. And you're feeling so relaxed and detached. Can you do that?

SUBJECT: [Breathes deeply] Yeah.

DAVID: Are you sure?

SUBJECT: Hmm, yes.

DAVID: I'm going to send some white light into you. Do you feel your body filling up with white, energetic light? Do you feel it coming down through your forehead? I want you to visualize this beautiful light and this love surrounding you now. Can you feel the love surrounding you now?

SUBJECT: I can feel it.

DAVID: Can you feel that?

SUBJECT: I can feel it.

DAVID: Now I want you to hold that love inside you in this beautiful bubble. You're surrounded with this beautiful bubble of light. You are just observing. You are not getting involved emotionally, and you're letting your body fill with love and light, always knowing that lives are to learn from and move on from after they're over. Not to take a life and absorb the negativity, but to learn from it, and move on, like the hundreds of other lives you have had. Isn't that right?

SUBJECT: Yeah.

DAVID: All right. Because the life of Laura and other lives are just one more of many lives, and this life has helped you to grow and evolve as a person, to make you the wonderful, beautiful person you are today. We all have lives. I've had many as well. So, I'm going to sit here and take us through this journey. How do you feel?

SUBJECT: I'm calm.

DAVID: Good. Well, at the age of fifteen, what year was that? Can you tell me the year and the date?

SUBJECT: [Pause] It was 1972.

DAVID: So, 1972. Do you see the month or the day?

SUBJECT: It was May.

DAVID: May. And what day did Laura leave? Do you remember?

SUBJECT: The first of May.

DAVID: So, it was May first?

SUBJECT: Yeah.

DAVID: 1972?

SUBJECT: Yeah.

DAVID: Now I want you to remain calm and relaxed. You feel the love and the light inside you, surrounded by a beautiful bubble. Do you feel it?

SUBJECT: Yeah.

DAVID: Do you know you're safe? Protected. So how did Laura's life end? Don't get emotional, just describe it to me. [Pause, waiting] And it's okay, whatever you say.

SUBJECT: She slit her wrists in the bathtub.

DAVID: [Softly] Was she sad?

SUBJECT: Yes. [Soft crying in background]

DAVID: Okay, I want you to let go of that emotion. Don't look at it. Let's get away from it. Let's not look at the scene anymore. I'm here with you. I want you to let it go and know that we learn from past lives. The things you're sharing are going to help other people, do you know that?

SUBJECT: I guess.

DAVID: The things you're sharing today are going to help other people in the future when they look at their lives now and the decisions they make. We're going to get away from that, and what is the next thing you see?

SUBJECT: [Breathes deeply]

DAVID: What do you see next? And don't get involved emotionally. Just let yourself go. Just keep yourself in the light. Just relax. And what do you see next after you've passed?

SUBJECT: I see my mom finding me.

DAVID: Okay, all right, don't look anymore. And were they upset? [Pause] We're just observing this life, alright?

SUBJECT: [Swallows] They were upset, but they could have helped me.

DAVID: They could have helped you in what way?

SUBJECT: My mom didn't listen to me.

DAVID: What do you mean, 'listen to you?' Give me more background on that. What did you tell her that she could have heard?

SUBJECT: She didn't listen to me when I told her about what was going on. [Swallows]

DAVID: And what was going on with Laura at this time? What upset you? [Pause]Can you tell me? We're just observing, and I'm here with you, holding your hand. So, all we're doing is recounting a life. We're not getting emotional. Can you do that?

SUBJECT: My stepbrother hurt me.

DAVID: You had a stepbrother?

SUBJECT: My parents got divorced when I was seven. And my mom remarried someone else. And he had two kids.

DAVID: So, your parents divorced when you were seven. What was your stepfather's name? What was his name?

SUBJECT: Richard.

DAVID: Did Richard live near your house on Cedar?

SUBJECT: My real dad was the one that left.

DAVID: And then Richard moved into your house?

SUBJECT: Yes.

DAVID: What was Richard's last name? Do you remember? [Pause] What was his last name?

SUBJECT: [Breathes deeply] Oh…

DAVID: Just take your time.

SUBJECT: O'Hare. O'Hare.

[Some readers may wonder why the questions I posed at this time seem to go off on a tangent from the death scene. Recounting a scene like that is very traumatic, and I felt it was best to bring the subject's mind away from it.]

DAVID: O'Hare, thanks. Now that you're older, you're fifteen. Now that you're older, you don't have to worry anymore about what the name of your town is. Can we look at that together? We're removed from all of this. So, I want you to remove yourself from the scene right now, and I want you now, as an older person, to give me the name of the town you lived in. Can you do that now? Since you're older and won't get in trouble? Since you're not five? Where was that street located? What town was your house in?

SUBJECT: [Breathes deeply] I can't see the whole name.

DAVID: Can you give me the letters again that you do see?

SUBJECT: C-O-N-S-T

DAVID: Good, but you can't see the next letter, huh?

SUBJECT: No. I don't know.

DAVID: Now let's go forward and get away from that life as Laura. Can we do that together?

SUBJECT: Okay.

DAVID: Now, let's go beyond that. Let's get away from that life, and let's look at where you are next. Once Laura left the earth, where do you see Laura next, after she left? Let's look at that. What do you see?

SUBJECT: [Pause] I stayed in my house for a long time.

DAVID: Did you? Now, I know sometimes it's hard to tell how long, but if you had to estimate in earth days or years, how long did Laura stay in the house? Roughly?

SUBJECT: Two years. Maybe three.

DAVID: Now is that because you were afraid to leave, or you just didn't know where to go? Why did Laura stay there?

SUBJECT: I couldn't leave.

DAVID: You what?

SUBJECT: I couldn't leave.

DAVID: And why couldn't Laura leave?

SUBJECT: I felt like I was trapped there.

DAVID: So, it felt like you were trapped there, and you didn't know where to go, is that correct?

SUBJECT: Yeah.

DAVID: Did it feel like you were kind of held there?

SUBJECT: Yeah.

DAVID: So, there were two to three years that Laura stayed around the house. Did you go outside of your house or just stay at your house mostly?

SUBJECT: [Sigh]

DAVID: And it's okay. We're not getting involved. We're just observing. And what did you do in the house? Do you remember?

SUBJECT: I tried… [Pause] I tried to communicate with my mom.

DAVID: To let her know you were still okay? You were still around?

SUBJECT: She blamed herself. She changed. She started drinking a lot, like my dad. I didn't want her to be sad.

DAVID: Your mom became sad and started drinking. What about the stepdad?

SUBJECT: She left him, my stepdad.

DAVID: She ended up leaving him?

SUBJECT: She left him. She was by herself.

DAVID: What was your mom's name again?

SUBJECT: Tracey.

DAVID: Where did Tracey go from there? Did she stay in that house or leave?

SUBJECT: She stayed.

DAVID: So, after your sad situation, you stayed in the house for another couple of years. How long after you were discovered did you stepfather move out? Was it in two months? Less than a year?

SUBJECT: Three months.

DAVID: And we don't have to discuss this. I think I already know the answer. So, you can just say 'yes' or 'no', you don't have to give me any details. Was the stepbrother abusing you?

SUBJECT: [softly] Yes.

DAVID: Okay, and we'll let it go at that. So, as they moved out, let's move forward. You were in the house, and your mother had started drinking more because she was sad she had lost Laura. And you stayed in the house because you felt trapped and wanted to stay there because your mother was there, and you tried to get in contact with her. Is that correct?

SUBJECT: Yes.

DAVID: Now when you stayed there two to three years, did your mom ever look around and feel, “I think I saw Laura”? Did she ever feel your presence?

SUBJECT: She did, but only when she was drunk.

DAVID: And how did you know that? How did you know she felt your presence when she was drunk?

SUBJECT: She would talk to me, and sometimes I felt like she could see me.

DAVID: So, she would get drunk, and it was easier to communicate with you when she was intoxicated, is that correct?

SUBJECT: Yes.

DAVID: Did it make you feel good that your mom was trying to contact you? Was it reassuring?

SUBJECT: Yeah, but it…

DAVID: But what?

SUBJECT: Yes, but it wasn't … it wasn't a good thing.

DAVID: So, you stayed there two to three years, and you stayed there because of your mother, and you felt bad. What did you do after those three years? Where did you go after that?

SUBJECT: When I first died, my grandma showed up. My grandma asked me if I was ready to go with her, but I said, "No." I said I didn't want to leave. And she said that when I was ready that she would come back or that I would just know where to find her. And so, I stayed, but I realized my mom couldn't move on, and she couldn't live her life if she was always looking for me, because I was already gone. And it wasn't fair like that. So, I left. I walked to the park my grandma used to take me to and she was there, and we left together.

DAVID: That's nice. Were you glad to see your grandmother again?

SUBJECT: Yeah.

[Understandably, the subject had a hard time moving on after witnessing her tragic ending. I decided to go back and re-examine her early responses, shifting her focus away from the tragedy.]

DAVID: Now was that your grandmother on your mother's side?

SUBJECT: Yeah, my mom's mom.

DAVID: And what was your grandmother's name? [Pause] Do you remember?

SUBJECT: Connie.

DAVID: Now let's think about this together. Your mother got married, and what was your last name again? When she got remarried?

SUBJECT: Um, Richard's name was O'Hare.

DAVID: Right, but what was your mom's married name?

SUBJECT: It was Guffy.

DAVID: Right, right. And your grandmother? What was her name again? I'm sorry.

SUBJECT: It was Constance, but everybody called her Connie.

DAVID: And what was Constance's last name?

SUBJECT: Hill or something with an I-L-L. It was a short name.

DAVID: So, in your mind you see grandma was named Connie Hill? Do you remember?

SUBJECT: Hill or Mills or something like that.

DAVID: Hill or Mills…got it. Well, you think about that. If it pops in your mind I want you to clarify that. Could you do that for me?

SUBJECT: Okay, Okay.

DAVID: Now, where did your grandmother go? Where did she take you?

SUBJECT: It felt like we were on an elevator, but there was no elevator. And the way that time feels, it doesn't feel the same when you're moving through it. It feels like you can take one single moment or second and stretch it out, like, to half a year or something and make it longer or make it shorter. And as soon as you don't want to be there anymore, you can leave the elevator.

DAVID: So, when you went in what felt like an elevator, did the doors open in some area at some time? How did that work? How did you know where to go? Did your grandmother take you where you needed to be?

SUBJECT: Yeah, she had my… she had my… shoulders. She was holding me. She had her arm around my shoulders.

DAVID: Oh, well that must have been pretty reassuring, wasn't it?

SUBJECT: Yeah, she told me that I needed to go and rest.

DAVID: Now, did she say goodbye to you for a while, so you could go rest?

SUBJECT: No, I went with her.

DAVID: Where did your grandmother take you to rest?

SUBJECT: We went to this place — it was kind of like a hospital, but not a hospital. It was like a place where people that are tired go when they're not living anymore, when something happened to them, or when they died suddenly or in a bad way. It's somewhere that they go so that they can recharge and learn and let go, so that they can move on.

DAVID: Sounds like a pretty nice place. A helpful place.

SUBJECT: Yeah.

DAVID: Now was your grandmother with you that whole time or did she say, "I'll be back"?

SUBJECT: No, she stayed with me.

DAVID: What was your name again?

SUBJECT: My name was Laura Guffy.

DAVID: Laura Guffy. And Laura, let me ask you this. And remember, we're just observing. We're just looking at that life as Laura. How long did it seem, if we can put a time on it — in earth time, how long were you in the hospital roughly?

SUBJECT: [Pause] Hmm. Years, but it felt like some of those years were really, really long and some of them were really short.

DAVID: So, time really wasn't like we know it. Is that right?

SUBJECT: Time is different than what we believe it to be.

DAVID: And who were the people that helped you? Were they nice and kind? What were they like, doctors and nurses here? If we could picture a doctor or nurse today in a hospital, what were they like on the other side?

SUBJECT: They all wore purple. Like purple doctors' outfits and nurses' outfits.

DAVID: So, they were all purple?

SUBJECT: Yeah, purple. Like lilac.

[Based on soul evolution colors, purple represents the highest attainable evolvement for a soul, right under the angel kingdom dimension, and GOD above that. It's understandable that highly evolved souls assist those with difficult and traumatic endings, no different than highly specialized doctors assisting patients here with psychological traumas.]

DAVID: And did they all seem like people that knew what they were doing? Souls that knew what they were doing?

SUBJECT: Yeah, they would do healing with us.

DAVID: Now as you were there, did they have names, or did they not have names, or names weren't important?

SUBJECT: I didn't know their names.

DAVID: Did you see anyone that we would know today on earth as far as saints or angels? Did anyone come to see you in the hospital?

SUBJECT: Gabriel came to see me. He's an angel.

DAVID: What was Gabriel like?

SUBJECT: He was very gentle. He…

DAVID: Was he very nice?

SUBJECT: He seemed like he was very compassionate, but that he wasn't the type of person or something that you would want to be on the bad side of.

DAVID: Okay, so he seemed very, very powerful, and you were glad he was on your side, is that right?

SUBJECT: Yeah.

DAVID: Describe what he looks like. How much bigger was he than, say, the purple doctors and purple nurses?

SUBJECT: He was really a lot taller than them.

DAVID: And what color was he? What did he radiate?

SUBJECT: He was gold. He glowed.

DAVID: Did he seem really, really powerful to you?

SUBJECT: I've never seen anything glow before, so yeah.

DAVID: So how did Gabriel come to the hospital? That's quite an honor or privilege to be able to meet an Archangel.

SUBJECT: Well, because Jesus was there.

DAVID: Say that again.

SUBJECT: Because Jesus was there.

DAVID: So, Jesus was at the hospital? He came to visit?

SUBJECT: Yeah, he was always there.

DAVID: So, you could always feel Jesus there, is that right?

SUBJECT: Yeah, but he was actually there.

DAVID: He was what?

SUBJECT: Yeah, but he wasn't just a feeling, he was really there.

DAVID: Okay, describe Jesus to me. Can you do that? What was he like?

SUBJECT: He had really, really nice, kind eyes. He smiled a lot. He had kind of crazy hair. It was longer, and it looked like he didn't brush it that much. And his beard looked like it didn't get brushed that much either. But you almost didn't notice that about him because he gave off some sort of energy that was really calming. He looked like he always was in a hurry when he got dressed in the morning too. He looked like he was messy.

DAVID: And what was he wearing?

SUBJECT: Um, he always wore just pants and a shirt, like a T-shirt, usually gray.

DAVID: So, when you saw him in the hospital he dressed in mostly gray pants and a shirt, but no robes or anything?

SUBJECT: No, but I knew it was him because of his hands.

DAVID: Because of his hands?

SUBJECT: Yeah, because his hands had scars.

DAVID: And did he say his name was Jesus or did you just know he was Jesus?

SUBJECT: I asked him who he was, and he took my hand, and he said that I knew who he was.

DAVID: And he had scars on his hands? Is that what you told me?

SUBJECT: Yeah, I could feel them.

DAVID: Did it feel like scar tissue?

SUBJECT: Yeah, it was raised on his bottom of his hand, on the heel of his hand.

DAVID: And what did it look like those scars were from?

SUBJECT: I knew what they were from.

DAVID: So, you knew that in the life as Laura before you came to this place, is that correct?

SUBJECT: Yeah, my grandma took me to church.

DAVID: Okay, now did Gabriel… you said Jesus was there a lot. Was Gabriel there as much or just once in a while?

SUBJECT: Just once in a while.

DAVID: What color were Jesus's eyes? Do you remember?

SUBJECT: They were dark. Maybe brown. But sometimes they looked brighter or something.

DAVID: Like they glowed somehow?

SUBJECT: Yeah, or just the type of eyes that feel soft.

DAVID: But knowing?

SUBJECT: Well, yeah, it's Jesus.

DAVID: Now you mentioned Gabriel and Jesus. Was there anyone else we might recognize today on earth? Any other saints or angels or figures from the bible we might recognize? Or is that pretty much the only two that we might recognize that came to you?

SUBJECT: Well, my grandma said that Mother Teresa ran some things there, but I never saw her. I didn't really know much about Mother Teresa.

DAVID: Okay, but you had heard about her from your grandmother that she had been there on occasions?

SUBJECT: Yeah, that's what I was told.

DAVID: Now looking at the hospital, did you float into it? Or were you just inside it all of the sudden once you got off the elevator?

SUBJECT: It's like I was just there.

DAVID: Like the elevator floor went right to it? Is that right?

SUBJECT: Yeah.

DAVID: And you stepped off with your grandmother. Were you a little surprised at what you saw?

SUBJECT: Yeah, I didn't think heaven was going to look like that.

DAVID: You didn't what?

SUBJECT: I didn't think heaven was going to look like that.

DAVID: So, when you arrived there, who came to see you first? Was it somebody in purple?

SUBJECT: Yeah, it was like a nurse or something, and…

DAVID: And did she know everything about you at that time before you said anything?

SUBJECT: Yeah, she said she had my case, and that she would show me where I was going to be, and that Jesus would come.

DAVID: Did you feel excited when you heard that Jesus would come?

SUBJECT: I don't think excited is the word for it.

DAVID: But it was quite an honor.

SUBJECT: I don't know. I didn't know what to expect.

DAVID: Right. So were you glad you had a chance to meet Jesus.

SUBJECT: I mean, yeah, who wouldn't?

DAVID: So, while you were in that hospital, and you were doing different things, and you'd met Jesus, and Archangel Gabriel came on occasion, you said time was sort of hard to pinpoint. And you mentioned that some of the years seemed like they were longer and some shorter, is that correct?

SUBJECT: Yeah.

DAVID: Now when you left the hospital, did your grandmother stay with you through the whole hospital experience?

SUBJECT: Yes, she worked there.

DAVID: Really? So, your grandmother worked at the hospital. That's pretty neat. Was she purple too?

[To reiterate: Purple is considered the highest evolution of a soul. The color denotes a soul that has had many lives, passed many tests, and has "graduated," in a sense, from Earth School or another of God's creations. All souls have a "color," starting at white and then, in order, pink, red, orange, yellow, green, blue, indigo and ending with purple. The colors overlap as a soul evolves, for example: a green eventually adding some blue as they evolve toward the next higher color. Similar to a spectrum or chakras, a soul advances through various stages in their soul evolution, earning advancing colors as they evolve. After eons, souls eventually attain the purple color designation meaning they're highly evolved.]

SUBJECT: Yeah.

DAVID: Well, that's nice having those connections.

SUBJECT: That's what she joked about.

DAVID: Those are connections. That's great. So that was a pretty important place and a pretty special place I think, would you agree?

SUBJECT: Yeah.

DAVID: So that's very nice. Your grandmother was there to help you and get you through this. And like you said, connections. And your grandmother laughed about that, is that what you said?

SUBJECT: Yeah, she used to joke about it.

DAVID: Did she say that this is a pretty special hospital, or place, or what?

SUBJECT: She told me that I was lucky to know friends in high places. She didn't say lucky though. She said I was blessed.

DAVID: Well, that's neat. That's very neat. Now after you left there, did your grandmother go with you and say, "-----------, it's time to go on, you're fine now," or how did that work?

SUBJECT: No, she didn't go with me. Jesus said that if I wanted to leave I could, but that if I didn't, I could stay.

DAVID: So, did you decide after a while, "I'll go somewhere else"? How long did you stay there do you think?

SUBJECT: I don't know. I stayed there until I went back to another life.

DAVID: You stayed in the hospital until you were ready to come back in another life?

SUBJECT: Yeah, because I didn't get to live that much.

DAVID: Yes, let's look at that. Did you come back pretty quick after that life? Do you remember?

SUBJECT: Well, yeah, I would say I did.

DAVID: Within ten or fifteen earth years maybe?

SUBJECT: I don't know if it was that few, but relatively speaking it was quickly.

DAVID: And after that life as Laura, what was your next life after that? Do you remember?

SUBJECT: Yeah, I came here.

DAVID: So, you came back as who you are today?

SUBJECT: Yeah.

DAVID: Okay, well, I am very impressed, and -------------, you are a very blessed person, that's for sure. And I'm happy that you're back as ------------. So out of that life as Laura, having those experiences, what do you think was the most important thing that you learned in that life? What did you learn?

SUBJECT: That I couldn't… I couldn't expect that suicide would ever solve anything for me.

DAVID: So, you realized that? That suicide wasn't the best choice?

SUBJECT: I… Yes, I knew that was the choice that I had made, and I couldn't change it, but I felt unfulfilled, because I took my own life. [Pause]. And so, when I decided to come back, I knew that I would have to have suffering again, so that I could learn how to overcome it and survive.

DAVID: Well, I think you've accomplished that.

SUBJECT: Well, I was lucky that I had my mom and dad now in this life.

DAVID: It's made it better, hasn't it?

SUBJECT: Yeah, when I was Laura I didn't have good parents.

DAVID: Well let's move on and go away from that life that you had as Laura and the lessons you learned: Your wonderful, strong grandmother, the opportunity to meet Archangel Gabriel and Jesus. Let's go down deeper and deeper and leave all the memories of that life, knowing that you learned from that life as Laura. Getting stronger now as -----------. Letting the pains and the hurt ebb out of the subconscious in the life as Laura, knowing you were there to learn. And you have learned.

We'll just float along. We'll just leave that all behind us. You're back in your beautiful bubble above the flowers, leaving it all behind. Just floating along. Just floating along. Not thinking about anything. Just letting your body drain the hurt and pain and feeling all the energy and love in your heart, knowing that you always have the love of Jesus and your grandmother, regardless of what life you're in, and that they're always there with you, as we found out on the other side in the hospital.

That strength and love is always with us regardless of the life we're in. And in the life of ------------- today, they're there for us even though we can't see them on earth. But from what we visualize in the heavenly realms and the hospital, we know those good souls are there to help us, there to guide us through this journey of life, if we just ask for their help. And they give us strength and protection. Does that seem like it makes sense to you?

SUBJECT: Mhmm…yes.

DAVID: Okay, well, stay in your bubble of light, just relaxed, and I'm going to count down from five to one again. Each time I count down, you're going to let go of all the bad memories, all the trauma, as you just float down, down, down. Getting more relaxed, more comfortable. Just floating down, down, down.

Knowing that we're here as souls to learn, to grow, and only through suffering do we learn the most. And I'll tell you that we know this, as Jesus showed us on the cross. The greatest lessons, the greatest wisdom only comes in suffering. That is the true path to wisdom. It is only through the feelings and the knowing gained through suffering is where we learn the most. And we gain much wisdom and experiences and learning in the process. Hard lessons we never could have duplicated in heaven, because we didn't live them there. Only here is it the hardest and accelerates our souls' growth. So that is the strength you have brought forth now and the energy that you have within you as a radiating being of light. A soul that has grown wiser and more knowledgeable as you go forth.

So, as you're floating along, just relaxing, catching your breath, feeling yourself just drifting. Back, above the sea of flowers. As you just float above the flowers, protected in love, knowing we will always have lessons in our lives, and each lesson makes us grow. Just like your grandmother's gone through in her lives. Many, many experiences, lives and lessons to get where she is. And that's why she's purple, because she's had the experiences and lives, and we're grateful for those above. Strive for that.

So, as you hear my voice we count from five to four, in this golden bubble of light as you float along. From four to three, just letting go and feeling so powerful now, because we know we live forever, we're immortal. And every time we come down to earth or another of God's creations for lessons that we take more of the wisdom back home with us as each journey adds something different. Finding ways to unlock the mysteries so that we can benefit and learn from our past.

And as we count from three to two, we know that the key to awakening is finding ourselves, and as Hermann Hesse told us, "The key to life is finding your self." Though the lessons or experiences might be hard at times, we know that they make us stronger in the end. Our way is forward. And through these experiences we learn, we grow. And we realize how strong we are, not getting ourselves caught up in the daily illusion of life. Living on the earth in the life, but also knowing that we have the ability to do things that we didn't think we could, and do lives in other places, and that's what we're here for. Share our worlds and journeys with others, our experiences, our love, and our wisdom. So that others can be helped on their journey.

So, as we count from two to one, drifting along in your beautiful bubble, right above the flowers in your mind. Just letting go. And knowing there will always be lives that aren't as memorable or pleasant to us as others. But we know that we learn from each one. There will always be balance; the Universal Laws support this. Learning in the process as we all do. And all of us have had hard lives at one time or another. It's only through living those lives that we can learn and experience and grow wiser on our path. Do you feel more relaxed now? Do you feel more carefree?

SUBJECT: No.

DAVID: Okay. And why don't you feel relaxed now? Tell me.

SUBJECT: [Pause] [Deep breath]

DAVID: Is it wanting to break through some of the memories we encountered and let those go? Let me know. How do you feel?

SUBJECT: [Deep breaths]

DAVID: And we know we have Jesus on our side, and we all will do things in lives we regret later, mistakes we made that we wish we didn't. But it does not define us. It is one life of many you've had. That's what I want you to remember. I want that to register throughout your whole core. In our lives we'll always make mistakes. If you feel that you made a mistake, it does not define you as a person or a soul. So, I want you to let go of all the doubt and all of the pain, realizing that the life as Laura is just one life of many you've had. Can you do that with me? Can you let it go? Can you still hear me?

SUBJECT: [Heavy breathing]

DAVID: ------------?

SUBJECT: Yes.

DAVID: Can you hear me? Can you let all of it go? Let it just exit you and flow out. Are you still dwelling on the life we just discovered?

SUBJECT: I'm still remembering it.

DAVID: I'm going to say one thing, and I want you to think very hard about this. No one is ever judged for mistakes. People make rash decisions that they regret, maybe. But the thing you have to remember is, as you noticed after you got off the elevator, who held your hand? Who said, "Look it's okay?" Who came to see you?

SUBJECT: [Whispered] Jesus.

DAVID: Yes, that's right, Jesus came. He does not hold it against you. He loves you. We will all have lives, many lives. All of us have made our share of mistakes. He knew that what happened to drive you to suicide was not your doing. You were very upset. You were young and acted impulsively because you hurt deeply. He knows all that. He knows all that. Jesus does not judge you, and don't forget Archangel Gabriel was there. And that's why your grandmother, with her highest level of soul color, purple, said, "Look Laura, we get it. Now let's just move on." Okay? You realize that, right?

SUBJECT: Yes.

DAVID: Jesus met you, right?

SUBJECT: Okay.

DAVID: So, I want you to let all that go. There's no reason to hold that pain. Just let it go. There's no reason to hold it. There's no reason to hold it anymore.

SUBJECT: Okay.

DAVID: I want you to let it all out, because Jesus forgave you. Did he not forgive you? He did, didn't he?

SUBJECT: Yeah.

DAVID: That's right. And who came to you? One of the top Archangels?

SUBJECT: Mhmm…yes.

DAVID: Do you know how rare that is? Very rare. And I'll be right up front with you, I have read hundreds of past life accounts from Dr. Michael Newton, Moody, Weiss, among others doing the type of work we're doing today, and their subjects rarely if ever meet Jesus or another ascended master, let alone an Archangel. This was a chance to get to know yourself better as ------------ in this life now. Jesus doesn't meet everyone that passes on. They might sense his presence, and it's rare from what I've heard to meet an Archangel, okay? So, you are a very special person. Do you know that?

SUBJECT: That's what my parents think. [Chuckles].

DAVID: Well, you are. And they know you're special. Your mother and dad know that you're special. Isn't that correct?

SUBJECT: Mhmm…yes.

DAVID: Well then you should be very proud of yourself, because that is something to be proud of. And when you leave today, what you want to come away with is not the life of Laura who tragically acted in an impulsive way when caught in a bad situation, not unlike thousands of people today who face tough situations. I have found in most cases it is easier for souls who are faced with hard lessons in a life to learn to overcome the hard lesson in the life they're living as opposed to having to come back and repeat it in another life.

You accepted these hard lessons before incarnating and it is a better idea to learn them the first time around, because you will have to pass them eventually in another life. And as you noticed with your mother, she started drinking as a result of your suicide, and by your actions you altered her path in a negative way. Those that take their own lives, or the lives of others, aren't often cognizant of who they damage in the process through their actions. That can lead to other karmic backlash as well that they aren't even aware of. The fact is that you were met and healed, and you stayed in that hospital until they felt you were ready to come back as ------------- or you wouldn't have come back. Do you know that?

SUBJECT: Mhmm…yes.

DAVID: God and Jesus had faith in you, as well as your grandmother or you wouldn't be here as ------------ right now. You would have taken maybe another thirty to hundred earth years or possibly longer to reincarnate again, right?

SUBJECT: Mhmm [yes].

DAVID: So, they know you're strong. They know you're ready. They know that was an accident. That's all. It was impulsive. It was done without a lot of thought. But you were fifteen and having a hard time. It's not unusual. I'm not saying you want to repeat it. You've learned from that, correct?

SUBJECT: Mhmm [yes].

DAVID: Good, you've learned from that, and that's what the lesson was all about. That's all. Because when you went into that life as Laura, you signed up for a hard life, did you know that?

SUBJECT: Mhmm [yes].

DAVID: And you came down and had a very hard life, right?

SUBJECT: Yeah.

DAVID: And you learned from that life, did you not?

SUBJECT: Yeah.

DAVID: A big chunk of life will be about lessons. Some lessons are painful, some good, some easy, some fun, and some horrific, right? It's about balance.

SUBJECT: Yeah.

DAVID: So, with that known, don't dwell on the life itself. Dwell on what you learned, how you grew from that experience.

SUBJECT: Okay.

DAVID: You just want to let it go. We all have tragic lives. But they're not all tragic. And that's why earth school has its good and bad. Sometimes you will have tougher lives than others. But each time we grow, we learn, do we not?

SUBJECT: Yeah.

DAVID: So that was just one learning experience, right?

SUBJECT: Yeah.

DAVID: How many lives do you think you've had? What number do you see pop into your head? What number?

SUBJECT: I don't know.

DAVID: Okay. Well, it's not important. But this is just one life of many you've had. It would be like opening a book of your lives and your records and having possibly a hundred or five-hundred different stories. Just one more story of many stories. Did you know that?

SUBJECT: Uh-uh [no].

DAVID: Well, that's how it works. Okay?

SUBJECT: Mhmm [yes].

DAVID: So, can we forget about that life? That was an accident and impulsive?

SUBJECT: Okay.

DAVID: Now let that go.

SUBJECT: [Sigh].

DAVID: I want you to be able to close your eyes and see that image of Jesus whenever you need him or Archangel Gabriel. Okay?

SUBJECT: Yeah.

DAVID: Because you've met them. They know ------------. They know all of ------------. They know all the lives of ------------. You know that, don't you?

SUBJECT: Yeah.

DAVID: And I promise you, your grandmother knows all the lives of ------------- and knows you. And it's not even just -------------, it's your soul. They all know you. You know that, right?

SUBJECT: I took care of my grandmother. I knew her. Again. I knew her again.

DAVID: In this life, or which life?

SUBJECT: Here.

DAVID: In this life?

SUBJECT: Yeah.

DAVID: Oh, you didn't tell me that. So, it's the same one? The same grandmother you think?

SUBJECT: Yeah, I know it was her.

DAVID: So, the one that helped you in the hospital, right?

SUBJECT: Yeah, Yeah.

DAVID: Connie, right?

SUBJECT: Yeah.

DAVID: Connie, what was her last name again?

SUBJECT: Hill or Mills.

DAVID: Hill or Mills. And in this life you returned the favor, didn't you?

SUBJECT: Yeah, I took care of her until she died.

DAVID: Isn't that amazing? How she was your grandmother in that life as Laura, and she came back in another incarnation before you, and you took care of her as an assistant in this life.

[This may seem confusing to some wondering how it was possible for the subject to know her grandmother as Laura in an earlier life, and as an older woman she helped as an assistant in this life. When a soul incarnates, there is always divine soul energy you leave on the other side and you are always connected when you splinter your energy. You are always connected to your higher self. So, what the subject experienced when she passed away as Laura was her grandmother's divine soul helping her on the other side. A reincarnating soul's energy needs when leaving the higher realms into a new life will determine how much of their divine soul energy is left on the other side. Harder lives usually require greater amounts of energy in earthly incarnations to handle more challenging experiences and lessons.]

SUBJECT: She wasn't my grandmother… she wasn't my grandma in this life.

DAVID: Okay, what was she?

SUBJECT: She was my grandma then, but she was someone else's grandma now: She was Mrs. Davis. Jill Davis. I just took care of her as an assistant.

DAVID: Her name was what?

SUBJECT: Her name was Jill Davis. That was her name.

DAVID: So, she was your grandma in the life as Laura, and an elderly woman you helped with needs in this life?

SUBJECT: Yes, she was someone I took care of. That's why… that's why it happened.

DAVID: Why, what happened?

SUBJECT: That's why I took care of her, because she took care of me.

DAVID: Sort of like a karma-type thing almost?

SUBJECT: Yeah, and I was supposed to find her again.

DAVID: So, you learned that on the other side before you came down as -----------, is that correct?

SUBJECT: Yeah, I think Jesus told me that.

DAVID: Jesus said that you would probably come down and take care of a Jill Davis?

SUBJECT: That I would take care of someone like my grandma that took care of me.

DAVID: And you think it was Jesus that told you that?

SUBJECT: I think so.

DAVID: Oh, well see how that works?

SUBJECT: Yeah.

DAVID: Pretty amazing how complex it is, isn't it?

SUBJECT: Well, it's not as complex as you could argue it to be. It's the laws of the universe.

DAVID: Now what else do the laws of the universe tell us that you remember that I'm not familiar with?

SUBJECT: Well, everyone is familiar with them; it's just how you apply them.

DAVID: Okay.

SUBJECT: For every action, there's a greater or equal reaction, that's a law. And everyone knows that, but it just looks different when you're not on earth.

DAVID: I want you to tell me a little more. So, on the other side, the laws are applied differently than what we know on earth, is that correct?

SUBJECT: Yes, not different, just applied differently.

DAVID: Okay.

SUBJECT: Earth is our whole world, but earth is not the entire world, if you know what I'm saying.

DAVID: Gotcha.

SUBJECT: It's just one part of … of a galaxy, inside of a universe, inside of other things. Everything is like … nesting dolls or something. It's complicated, and it took time to make it the way that it is, and everything has to fit inside of everything else.

DAVID: That's very interesting. And you knew before you came back, that your parents in this life would be your parents?

SUBJECT: Yeah, and I knew my dad before.

DAVID: Was that in some other life in the past with him?

SUBJECT: Yeah, I think he was… yeah, I think he was in my family in another life.

DAVID: That's very interesting. Is there anyone else in this life?

SUBJECT: My cousin, I knew my cousin.

DAVID: Your cousin?

SUBJECT: Yeah, I knew him, and there was a guy that I dated in college that I knew.

DAVID: You feel pretty good about that, right?

SUBJECT: Yeah, he knew me. He knew me in a way that we couldn't possibly have known. I mean, we had only just met.

DAVID: So, when you look at the hospital, even though you went in something like an elevator from that park…

SUBJECT: It wasn't an elevator, that's just what it felt like.

DAVID: Right, because it felt like you were zooming up?

SUBJECT: Yeah, it was the same sensation.

DAVID: Right, so what, like a physical—

SUBJECT: No, not really.

DAVID: So, it's just like all of a sudden you felt yourself rising up fast, right?

SUBJECT: Mhmm...yes.

DAVID: Now, when you got to the hospital, would that be considered still on our earth plane?

SUBJECT: I don't think so. It didn't feel like earth. Everything was different.

DAVID: Do you think it was because it was in a lighter dimension, like heaven?

SUBJECT: Yeah, that's what it felt like.

DAVID: But you don't think it was on this planet?

SUBJECT: No.

DAVID: In a lighter dimension?

SUBJECT: Yes, but I think it was somewhere else.

DAVID: Were there a lot of patients in the hospital? Can I ask you that?

SUBJECT: It wasn't crowded, but it wasn't empty either.

DAVID: And was it hard to measure how big it really was?

SUBJECT: Yeah, I can't… I can't really quantify it with words.

DAVID: It was just so big and massive, right?

SUBJECT: Well, there are a lot of people in the universe.

DAVID: Yeah, so that's what you noticed. Okay. Were there people from other universes besides earth? Or other star systems?

SUBJECT: I don't know, but I think… I think that there were.

DAVID: You thought that maybe some weren't from our planet?

SUBJECT: Not where I was, but it didn't feel like we were on our planet, so I guess it's possible.

DAVID: Were other people there who had a tragic ending that you met?

SUBJECT: Yeah, I met people that had also killed themselves or been murdered or died from sickness or things like that.

DAVID: Things that were traumatic, right?

SUBJECT: Yeah, things that they didn't really want.

DAVID: I understand. Did you have things like group meetings and stuff?

SUBJECT: I wasn't into it… Well, my grandma wanted me to go to them, but I told her I wasn't going to group meetings. I thought it was silly. I just didn't like talking in them. I talked to people outside of that, but I didn't like the idea of group therapy in heaven, if you will.

DAVID: So you didn't like group therapy in heaven?

SUBJECT: Yeah, it felt stupid.

DAVID: So, you just kind of learned things on your own with your grandmother's help?

SUBJECT: Yeah, I decided I didn't want to be in group therapy where I would be a victim and have to be treated like a victim. I wanted to help other people, and so I did.

DAVID: So, after you'd been there a while, they let you talk to other people who just came in and you said, "Hi, I'm Laura, welcome"?

SUBJECT: Yeah, I was like their welcome committee or something.

DAVID: So, you made them feel better, kind of like your grandmother did for you?

SUBJECT: Yeah, I would help them get settled.

DAVID: Well that was nice. And you enjoyed that job right, because you felt like it was doing good things for those that had…?

SUBJECT: I liked it better than sitting in group therapy.

DAVID: So, did you have to sleep? You said you went to rest.

SUBJECT: Yeah, but it felt more like we were in meditative states, not necessarily sleep.

DAVID: So, you just relaxed and let yourself go, but not like sleeping here?

SUBJECT: No, more like a trance.

DAVID: And that helped you reenergize, right?

SUBJECT: Yeah.

DAVID: Did they ever put you in any type of a machine or a pyramid or anything to reenergize or help boost your energy with sound and lights?

SUBJECT: I don't know, but a lot of my freckles and moles on my skin are triangle-shaped. They all connect together to make triangles.

DAVID: Okay, but you don't remember personally going inside a pyramid of glass or crystal and sitting inside it?

SUBJECT: No, but there were crystals there.

DAVID: There were crystals there?

SUBJECT: Yeah.

DAVID: Big ones? What kind? What are we talking about?

SUBJECT: They were mostly clear or a little bit cloudy, but it was like the walls were made of them.

DAVID: So, you could walk into a room lined with crystals, and it felt like they had energy coming out of them?

SUBJECT: Mhmm…yes.

DAVID: Did it felt almost like going under, not a good comparison, but let's say you know how some people use tanning beds in winter to get a good feeling?

SUBJECT: Not like that. It was more like sunlight.

DAVID: So, it was more like sunlight that was coming in and hitting you.

SUBJECT: Yeah, like sitting in a window and the sun is shining in.

DAVID: It felt good right?

SUBJECT: Yeah.

DAVID: Now, did you have a window in your room?

SUBJECT: I think so.

DAVID: What did you do in the room when you were done greeting people and doing other things?

SUBJECT: I didn't really sit around much.

DAVID: So, you were always moving unless you were in a trance state?

SUBJECT: Yeah.

DAVID: So, you would go into your room and…go into a trance state or where would you go?

SUBJECT: I could just do it wherever I was.

DAVID: So, you could just do it wherever. Were you floating around in a body again?

SUBJECT: No, I could if I wanted to, but I didn't all the time.

DAVID: Did you have a human form?

SUBJECT: Yeah.

DAVID: So, you pretty much had a human form. Was it like Laura when you left?

SUBJECT: Yeah, but I made myself look a little bit different, and I didn't keep the scars on my wrists. I didn't keep my wounds.

DAVID: Okay.

SUBJECT: Some people did. Some people chose too. Like when you're in… they tell you there's no pain in heaven, and there's no crying and no suffering. Well that's true, but sometimes for people that died a certain way, you could still see how they died. If their head got blown off you could see the scar around their head or something like that. But if they chose to make it go away or make it look different, they could.

DAVID: So, they had the ability to remove their wounds from another life?

SUBJECT: Their disfiguration, I guess.

DAVID: But some decided to keep them?

SUBJECT: Some people kept them as a way to help other people. I don't really understand that approach but… I don't know.

DAVID: Well that is amazing information. So, Jesus, when you saw him on the other side, was the kind of person who didn't care about his appearance as much in a sense. His hair and beard were not as much a concern as helping others, is that correct?

SUBJECT: Yeah, he just looked kind of disheveled all the time. But it was endearing in, you know, a funny way.

DAVID: And Gabriel, what did he look like? You told me he was tall, but what did he look like?

SUBJECT: I could never really see his face very well.

DAVID: Was he just like a big, golden ball of energy?

SUBJECT: He had a form, but he wasn't, you know, he wasn't necessarily really defined.

DAVID: But you could sort of see an image inside this energy?

SUBJECT: Yeah, and apparently that's how God can be when God is in a room or your presence is there with God.

DAVID: Were you able to consciously play music, or was there music in the hospital?

SUBJECT: There was a sound, like a vibration all the time.

DAVID: So, there was a constant vibration?

SUBJECT: Yeah.

DAVID: And it was like that all the time?

SUBJECT: Yeah, it was like music but not like music that you've ever heard.

DAVID: All right, sort of a hard-to-describe vibration? Would it be, and maybe you don't know this, but was it around 430-440 hertz or did you have any idea? Perhaps in the heart chakra range?

SUBJECT: I don't know how to gauge it.

DAVID: Where did it hit you when you were there? Throughout your whole body?

SUBJECT: You felt it in your chest.

DAVID: Mostly, in your chest?

SUBJECT: Your chest and throat.

DAVID: Isn't that interesting. Well, if you're ready, I'm ready to count up. Have we learned a lot?

SUBJECT: Yeah.

DAVID: And you have shared a lot. And through your strengths and your sharing, we may be able to help others with this information. Does that sound like a good cause?

SUBJECT: Yeah.

DAVID: Your story may help others to see, that impulsive decisions are not the way to make things better most of the time. Thinking through one's actions carefully before acting on them is usually a better idea. Does that make sense?

SUBJECT: Yeah.

DAVID: Okay. Well let's count up from one to five and each time I count up this time you'll start to wake up. You're going to wake up a little more each time, does that sound good?

SUBJECT: Okay.

DAVID: And you're going to be full of energy. You now know that in your mind you met Jesus. Anytime you feel down, sad, insecure, scared, fearful, you can visualize what you have now experienced…that you have the power of reaching out your hand, and having Jesus take yours. Do you realize that now?

SUBJECT: Yeah.

DAVID: You didn't know that before, did you?

SUBJECT: I don't know if I knew it exactly, but…

DAVID: Well, I think we all have felt Jesus personally if we want to. There is a Jesus for us in our times of need. But you've actually visualized him, which most people never have. And you also met Archangel Gabriel, which I think is very special, to say the least. And you know he's around too. So that's good. That's something that you can hold in your mind. If you can hold anything of this time, hold those images — those and your grandmother, and the lady you helped here in this life, and the work you did on the other side by helping others settle in. These are all big, big things. Okay?

SUBJECT: Okay.

DAVID: Let's not dwell on the impulsive behavior of a young, abused adolescent. Just let that go. That's not important. What is important is what you've learned. Isn't that correct?

SUBJECT: Mhmm…yes.

DAVID: And that's past us; that's gone. That's flying out — all that pain you might have been holding without knowing it in your subconscious. All that fear, all that sadness, float it out. Replace it with the love you've felt from your grandmother, from Jesus, from Archangel Gabriel, and feel their power come into you. That's all you have to take back. Frankly, that's a heck of a gift. So, you can visualize that in your mind, erasing all the negative, emotional energies from that life as Laura. Knowing you are stronger, knowing it's one life of hundreds you have had.

Let's go up from one to two. Rising up. Starting to feel your toes wiggle around. Feeling more warmth coming down through you. As we count from two to three, feeling yourself taking a little more of a breath, stretching a little more. Rising from three to four. Starting to move your legs and feeling stronger as a result and well rested, like you just took a ten-hour nap. Feeling all this energy. Not that you won't sleep tonight. But as you awaken, you feel the energy flowing down through you, knowing you have the power and that you were just recounting another life of many you've had, which is good. We're all here for lessons. And through lessons and experiences we know more about ourselves, we know the love that's waiting for us, as we stretch from four to five. Letting it all go. Just stretching, getting comfortable, waking up. Breathing in and out.

Healing Pain and Life Review as an 1800's Mother

A woman in her mid-thirties came to me wanting to do a past life regression and mentioned she also had physical pain. I inquired about stomach issues after she touched her stomach several times and grimaced. Follow along as she recounts a tough life living in the 1800's, and the process she experienced reviewing that life with her council.

DAVID: We're doing a reading today. And we're going to work on various health issues in addition to the IBS. What are other health issues you are experiencing?

SUBJECT: I just don't know what's going on with my stomach. Honestly, more just the emotional stuff. Just… cutting the connections to the negative beings in my life, if that's okay.

DAVID: Well, we can do that, anything else?

SUBJECT: No.

DAVID: Okay, remove stress and anxiety as well as stomach issues. Bring a big sense of calm and power. And bring in more positive people.

SUBJECT: Just not to have the negative people in my life able to affect me the way they do.

DAVID: Gotcha. Sort of like a shield-type thing.

SUBJECT: Yes.

DAVID: And, of course, the stomach. What about the lower-back, anything?

SUBJECT: Nope.

DAVID: Okay, so I'd like you to get comfortable…

[As there was pain and emotional turmoil present, I took her very deeply into a hypnotic state. Often, when the pain, whether emotional or physical, is strong, it requires going not only in to the subconscious recesses of the mind but inducing a super-conscious state. This state also heightens the past life regression experience, life between lives recall, and in some instances, an opportunity to experience an end of life review by one's Council of Elders. Her council had some good advice for her.]

DAVID: Feeling so relaxed and so happy inside as you drift down deeper and deeper. Feeling yourself in the bubble. So how do you feel?

SUBJECT: Relaxed.

DAVID: So, as you drift down just enjoying the moment, you begin to notice your mind's eye opening. Absorbing this golden, peaceful light, not too overwhelming, but powerful. As you drift down deeper and deeper, more and more relaxed, you're starting to get closer to the ground. You're drifting down toward the base of an enormous tree that you are floating alongside of in your bubble, almost like a leaf falling gently off a tree, so relaxed, so peaceful.

[Only when writing this book and reading through the transcribed recording did I pick up on the metaphor I used in the hypnotic induction: the action of a leave falling off of a tree, just gently floating down. It is a way to symbolize death and the release experienced by a soul when they pass on and depart from "the tree of life."]

DAVID: The tree is surrounded by flowers that are all around its base, and you're drifting along. Just drifting along now, away from the tree. And you're floating about ten to fifteen feet above this beautiful field of flowers. It's just a sea of wild flowers, and you feel yourself just drifting along, down into little valleys and up little hills, just drifting along above the beautiful flowers. Just going with the flow, knowing you're guided and loved by Divine energy. Allowing the energy to steer the way as you drift along, feeling yourself just gently wafting along on the breeze. You're in this beautiful light. And you can see through the bubble, it's translucent, but maybe a little murky, a little glossy at first, like something is on the outside of it.

[The "murky" or glossy reference used in this case is to describe the possibility that the pictures and visions that came to her initially wouldn't be totally clear. This is not unusual to experience when exploring a new life. These memories of a former life are locked deeply away. It's similar to going into an old attic and discovering forgotten photo albums that may be worn, yellowed, faded and dusty and recounting memories of your childhood many years later.]

But you're beginning to see in your mind, because your eyes are closed, as you drift along. You know you're drifting along over this bed of beautiful, different colored wild flowers. And as we count down from five to four, you feel yourself drifting down even further down.

As you're drifting along above the sea of flowers, you know they don't last forever, and you're starting to feel like you're coming to the edge of the flowers, which is fine. You want to move forward and now explore and learn new things about yourself. And as you drift along, gently along, as we count down to three, you're sinking deeper and deeper. In your mind's eye as you drift along across the flowers, you begin to visualize a house or structure in your mind. Beginning to see in your mind somewhere before that you might have liked or enjoyed. It goes back to a more ancient time, a time long ago.

And as you're drifting along in this bubble, you can see not only a familiar house or structure, you also start to see a town or a community as you drift above it. You start to get an idea, and you let that image develop in your mind. You can feel yourself opening up to another time, another life, a life which will help you now in this life and give you some ideas of how to move this life forward. And you let this picture develop, not rushing what you're starting to see, because it might be fuzzy or hazy early on. Just letting it develop in your mind's eye. Perhaps there are certain smells or sounds around. Maybe the outside air is a certain temperature.

You're just observing and wanting to enjoy this experience from your past. You feel all safe and secure, because you are. We have angels all around us, allowing you to enjoy this experience of past times. So, as you begin to leave this bubble, you'll come out of your bubble, and I want you to stand on the edge of a hill looking down at this house or community.

And as we count down to two you're going to feel the images getting even stronger, starting to remember other people in that life, other names. And as we drift down to one, you feel the pictures getting stronger. You feel that you might know who you are as you observe everything around you. Drifting down deeper and deeper, you feel the images getting stronger and the memories getting stronger. And now you see it in your mind.

SUBJECT: [Gentle snoring]

DAVID: ------------, do you notice anything in your mind?

SUBJECT: I'm just relaxed.

DAVID: So, you're not seeing any images of houses or anything?

SUBJECT: Uh-uh [no].

DAVID: So, as you're relaxing, do you feel all the pain exiting your body?

SUBJECT: Mhm [yes].

DAVID: Feeling it all go away?

SUBJECT: Yes.

DAVID: Do you want to visualize a past life? Do you want to try?

SUBJECT: Mhm [yes].

[At this stage, though the client felt the pain exiting her body, she didn't appear to be deep enough to complete a past life regression.

I decided to use some deepening hypnotic techniques to allow for this.]

DAVID: [Ending deepening hypnotic techniques] So, while you're relaxing I want you to hear my voice and listen to what I say. Listen to my questions, and let's see if we can build some images in your mind of another life.

And now, you just stepped out of your golden bubble, and you are protected. You're just observing this life, and you are looking straight ahead. Perhaps the images show up like they're on a projector screen and they're starting to take on a three-dimensional look. You see yourself standing there and gazing, starting to see in your mind's eye things that are familiar to you. You're seeing images in your mind's eye very clearly now. They're getting brighter and brighter, clearer and clearer. Are you seeing images that relate to you and your past?

SUBJECT: Mhm [yes].

DAVID: Describe to me what you see.

SUBJECT: It's a ball of light.

DAVID: The structure is a ball of light?

SUBJECT: Yes, it's far away.

DAVID: Okay.

SUBJECT: It's very dark out here.

DAVID: Now what is this ball of light? Is it similar to a miniature sun or do people live on it?

SUBJECT: I don't know what it is.

DAVID: And where are you in relation to this ball of light?

SUBJECT: Just sitting, waiting for it to come to me.

DAVID: As you're sitting there waiting on this ball to come to you, can you send messages to it that you're ready? Telepathically? How do you communicate?

SUBJECT: I'm telling it to come to me telepathically.

DAVID: So, you're sitting there waiting and waiting. Now, how long have you known of this ball of light?

SUBJECT: I don't know, a long time.

DAVID: As you see this ball of light, do you remember it coming to you as a child?

SUBJECT: Mhm [yes].

DAVID: And as you look at this ball of light, do you ever go inside of it?

SUBJECT: No.

DAVID: So, it comes to you and talks to you, I guess? Telepathically?

SUBJECT: Mhm [yes].

DAVID: And what do you talk about? Do you remember a few things? Do they tell you where they're from or anything?

SUBJECT: We talk about my experiences.

DAVID: In this life now or another life?

SUBJECT: It's another, but they're with me at the end of all my lives. It's not my spirit guide, but they're an important person.

DAVID: So, this ball of light is a soul and helps you in a lot of lives?

SUBJECT: Mhm [yes].

DAVID: Now did you die and that's why you're here?

SUBJECT: Uh-uh [no].

DAVID: You did not. So, you're alive in that life and you still had this golden ball of light come to you, is that correct?

SUBJECT: Mhm [yes].

DAVID: Did the golden ball of light go to others, or don't you know?

SUBJECT: I don't know. I didn't ask.

DAVID: Did you ever feel like… why did they pick you? Did they ever tell you?

SUBJECT: No. I just think that I'm part of the group. I'm part of the group.

DAVID: Well, that sounds interesting. So, as you're observing this life and seeing this ball as it's coming toward you, and you feel so relaxed, do you feel like you're on earth as you're waiting for the ball?

SUBJECT: Uh-uh [no].

DAVID: Where do you think you are?

SUBJECT: I don't know.

DAVID: Do you think you're on another planet?

SUBJECT: No. It's just a building.

DAVID: It's a building?

SUBJECT: With lots of doors down the hallway.

DAVID: And you're waiting in this building, is that right?

SUBJECT: Mhm [yes].

DAVID: So, you see the building, what is this building?

SUBJECT: I don't know what I'd call it. It's just like a hallway with doors.

DAVID: Okay, but you're inside this building in another life?

SUBJECT: Mhm [yes].

DAVID: And how old does the building look? Does it look old?

SUBJECT: Old.

DAVID: Think of what you know about architecture, because you've seen a lot of houses and old buildings in your life: Does it look like it's from the early 1900s or what year do you think?

SUBJECT: Way before that.

DAVID: Can you give me a rough estimate of the timeframe?

SUBJECT: This is the 1800s.

DAVID: Sometime in the 1800s?

SUBJECT: Mhm [yes].

DAVID: Mid-1800s? Do you think Lincoln was around then or not?

SUBJECT: Mhm [yes]. Before Lincoln.

DAVID: So, it was a big building that had a lot of doors and it was old. What was the outside made of?

SUBJECT: Brick.

DAVID: And there were a lot of horse and buggies, I guess?

SUBJECT: Mhm [yes].

DAVID: Is that how you got around?

SUBJECT: Mhm [yes].

DAVID: Did you have a job in this building?

SUBJECT: Uh-uh [no].

DAVID: So, why were you in the building?

SUBJECT: I don't know. I was meeting people to talk.

DAVID: You were seeing other people there?

SUBJECT: Mhm [yes].

DAVID: So, you didn't work in that building, but did you have any type of a job in that life?

SUBJECT: No.

DAVID: You did not have a job?

SUBJECT: I was a mom.

DAVID: You were a mom. And that means you were married, right?

SUBJECT: Mhm [yes].

DAVID: And you had kids?

SUBJECT: Mhm [yes].

DAVID: How many?

SUBJECT: Four.

DAVID: What were their names?

SUBJECT: [Mumbled] I don't know.

DAVID: Can you see them in your mind?

SUBJECT: Uh-uh [no].

DAVID: But you knew you had four children, correct?

SUBJECT: Mhm [yes].

DAVID: And where did you live? Because this is back in what, 18… Does it feel like mid-1800s? Like 1850s? Or what?

SUBJECT: It's just a long time ago. It's really dark.

DAVID: So, as you remember that life, do you remember what state you lived in?

SUBJECT: Uh-uh [no].

DAVID: Well, let's concentrate on the family. Can you see the house you lived in?

SUBJECT: Mhm [yes].

DAVID: Can you describe the house to me?

SUBJECT: It's stone. It has a porch.

DAVID: And what else? Can you walk inside and tell me what you see?

SUBJECT: [Long pause] There's a fireplace and chairs made out of wood, homemade chairs. There's an archway, and through the archway there's a room, and there's bed-like stuff.

DAVID: Did you like the house?

SUBJECT: Mhm [yes].

DAVID: Did it stay pretty warm in the winter?

SUBJECT: No. It wasn't very big. There was a fireplace.

DAVID: So that helped keep you warm?

SUBJECT: Mhm [yes].

DAVID: So, what else did you use the fireplace for?

SUBJECT: Cooking, boiling water to take baths.

DAVID: Did you have a cast iron tub or something? How did you do that? What did the tubs look like back then?

SUBJECT: Just a big pot that I boiled water in.

DAVID: So, you'd take a bath in a big pot?

SUBJECT: Yeah, it wasn't like a tub. Not a pot, not like a regular tub, but like a tub.

DAVID: Right. Now did you remember a lot of snows while you were there? Did it ever snow?

SUBJECT: No. It was…

DAVID: So, it didn't snow a lot?

SUBJECT: It wasn't snowing now.

DAVID: Do you remember any snows when you lived in the house? Or winters weren't that cold and snowy?

SUBJECT: They're not that bad.

DAVID: So, you probably lived somewhere in the south, is that correct?

SUBJECT: Mhm [yes].

DAVID: What state in the south do you think you were from?

SUBJECT: Nothing. Just territories.

DAVID: Oh, so they weren't even states yet, just territories.

SUBJECT: [Sigh] Yes.

DAVID: Was it near the Atlantic Ocean or the Gulf? What do you remember? What was the closest water?

SUBJECT: There's a river, but it's not extremely close.

DAVID: So, you weren't close to the ocean then?

SUBJECT: No.

DAVID: Or the Gulf, right?

SUBJECT: No.

DAVID: And by horseback that would be a heck of a journey, correct?

SUBJECT: Yes.

DAVID: Were they starting to run any railroads near you? [Pause] Do you remember?

SUBJECT: Uh-uh [no].

DAVID: So, they weren't running any steam locomotives or anything near you with big whistles and all that?

SUBJECT: There was kind of a station near me. There's something. A station.

DAVID: I want you to continue to remember that life and continue to think about it. As we count down, you're drifting down deeper and deeper, feeling the images open up even more. You're seeing your four children, starting to realize which are the boys and girls.

SUBJECT: Three boys, one girl.

DAVID: And you're starting to see names in your head?

SUBJECT: Uh-uh [no].

DAVID: Do you feel like you might know your first name?

SUBJECT: No, I'm very confused.

DAVID: So, you don't know what your name is?

SUBJECT: Uh-uh [no].

DAVID: That's okay. We're just reviewing the life. You had three sons and a daughter, right?

SUBJECT: Uh-huh [yes].

DAVID: And was your husband a pretty good guy?

SUBJECT: He wasn't around much. He worked.

DAVID: He worked hard?

SUBJECT: Mhm [yes].

DAVID: Well, that's good, at least he brought in food for the family, right?

SUBJECT: Mhm [yes].

DAVID: It's very important. So, I'm glad. As we count down deeper and deeper. Feeling yourself, just opening up even wider. Seeing these images all around. Seeing them playing in front of you. Seeing yourself just observing, as you go forward in that life. As you drift down, down, the images get brighter and brighter, much easier to see, describe and remember. And as you drift down you're seeing the images expand. Let's go forward in that life; do you see yourself as an older woman?

SUBJECT: Mhm [yes].

DAVID: So, you see yourself as an older woman. Are you feeling older and more tired?

SUBJECT: Mhm [yes].

DAVID: Raised a good family, right? You felt pretty happy with that?

SUBJECT: I was happy.

DAVID: As you're drifting along, how do you feel you were as a mother?

SUBJECT: I was a good mom.

DAVID: Were you a good cook?

SUBJECT: Mhm [yes].

DAVID: As you're drifting along, remembering that life, feeling and seeing yourself getting older and older… Were you happy in that life?

SUBJECT: I sit by the fireplace a lot. It makes me happy.

DAVID: Do you read any books or just rock?

SUBJECT: I rock, I cook.

DAVID: Are you still in the same house?

SUBJECT: Mhm [yes].

DAVID: So, have you been in that house for a very long time?

SUBJECT: Mhm [yes].

DAVID: And you like your house, and you like that fireplace?

SUBJECT: Mhm [yes].

DAVID: What was your favorite dish to cook?

SUBJECT: Cornbread.

DAVID: Were you pretty good at cornbread?

SUBJECT: Mhm [yes].

DAVID: Where did you get your meat?

SUBJECT: From livestock.

DAVID: Did you raise livestock?

SUBJECT: No, other people in the town did.

DAVID: What about milk? How did you get milk?

SUBJECT: Yes, we had milk cows.

DAVID: So, did you make butter and cheese?

SUBJECT: Mhm [yes].

DAVID: I want you to visualize yourself in that past life. You're by the fireplace. You're feeling the warmth of the fire. You're gently rocking back and forth, realizing you had a long life. And how old were you when you died?

SUBJECT: I was old. My face was all wrinkled.

DAVID: So, you're pretty old, but you don't remember the exact year?

SUBJECT: No. My hair is gray.

DAVID: What do you look like?

SUBJECT: I look frail. Like a little frail grandma…tiny…very tiny. I'm small. I'm not tall.

DAVID: Not tall, pretty small. Feeling very frail. The fireplace is nice, but you know you're time is coming close, right?

SUBJECT: It was where I was happy.

DAVID: And you were very happy, weren't you?

SUBJECT: I watched the children play.

DAVID: You'd watch them play, and you watched them grow up, right?

SUBJECT: Mhm [yes].

DAVID: Now, right before you passed, did you have a lot of grandchildren?

SUBJECT: Mhm [yes].

DAVID: Did you have great grandchildren?

SUBJECT: Mhm [yes].

DAVID: So, quite a big family, right?

SUBJECT: Mhm [yes].

DAVID: And you were the start of a lot of that.

SUBJECT: Mhm [yes].

DAVID: So, you felt pretty happy about how things all worked out, right?

SUBJECT: Mhm [yes].

DAVID: It sounds very nice. Well, as you get older, you had a good life, and I want you to go right to your death. How did you die?

SUBJECT: [Whispered] I just died.

DAVID: Were you in bed?

SUBJECT: I was asleep in the rocker. I just drifted off.

DAVID: So, it was a nice, peaceful death, right? You just kind of drifted off?

SUBJECT: Mhm [yes].

DAVID: And as you drifted off, and as you're seeing yourself, you continue to remember these images. Did you see yourself come out of your body? Your spirit?

SUBJECT: Yes.

DAVID: Were you standing in the room right when you died?

SUBJECT: Mhm [yes].

DAVID: How long did you stay there?

SUBJECT: My husband joined me. My husband came to join me, and we left together.

DAVID: You're husband came to join you?

SUBJECT: He came to get me.

DAVID: He had already passed away?

SUBJECT: Yes.

DAVID: How long before you did he pass away?

SUBJECT: Not long. Three years, four years.

DAVID: So, your husband came and met you right when you passed away?

SUBJECT: Mhm [yes].

DAVID: Well, that was very nice. Were you glad to see him again?

SUBJECT: Mhm [yes]. I was very content with this life. When he came to get me, I didn't want to fight. I was ready to go.

DAVID: Well, it sounds like a wonderful life. When your husband came for you, where did you go? Where did he take you?

SUBJECT: To go meet with everyone.

DAVID: So, you went to meet with everyone?

SUBJECT: Mhm [yes].

DAVID: Where did he take you to meet them? What did it look like?

SUBJECT: [Mumbles]

DAVID: Say that again?

SUBJECT: I see different colors. There is a lot of white lights. There's purple lights. There's blue lights. There's green lights. There's … golden light.

DAVID: So, about every color you can think of, I guess.

SUBJECT: There are a couple of red lights. But I stay away from them.

DAVID: A couple of what color?

SUBJECT: Red.

DAVID: And you stay away from red?

SUBJECT: Mhm [yes].

DAVID: Why would you avoid red?

SUBJECT: I just don't like them.

DAVID: You don't feel comfortable around red?

SUBJECT: No, they make me uncomfortable.

DAVID: Well, that's interesting. And when you see all those beautiful colors out there, are those all souls?

SUBJECT: Mhm [yes].

DAVID: Their soul color shows their evolution and everything. You kind of know… There's no secrets, is that correct?

SUBJECT: No secrets.

DAVID: So, everything is known, is that right?

SUBJECT: Yes.

DAVID: So, whatever color a person is, you're not going to fool somebody else by having a different color…

SUBJECT: No.

DAVID: It's all very regulated, isn't it?

SUBJECT: Yes.

DAVID: Tell me about heaven, where you are, because it sounds like you're in heaven. When your husband brought you there to meet others, who else did you meet when you arrived?

SUBJECT: Just him.

DAVID: Just him? No other deceased relatives?

SUBJECT: No. We were just kind of going at our own pace, while everybody else was with… the other lights…

DAVID: So, when you arrived, it was like everybody was doing their own thing and you and your husband just went and did your own thing too, I guess?

SUBJECT: No, we're going somewhere; we're just taking our time.

DAVID: You have somewhere you need to go but you're taking your time getting there, just to get used to it, is that correct?

SUBJECT: Mhm [yes].

DAVID: And where are you going to go after taking your time to get there?

SUBJECT: [Mumbles] Go in to talk to the wise ones.

DAVID: I'm sorry?

SUBJECT: Go and talk to the wise ones.

DAVID: So, you're going to talk to the wise ones with your husband?

SUBJECT: Mhm [yes].

DAVID: Now are these the ones that helped you with your soul contract or lessons in this life before you incarnated?

SUBJECT: Yes.

DAVID: Is this a council? What are you going to see them concerning?

SUBJECT: It is my Council and we're going to discuss the life I just had.

DAVID: Go over the things you did?

SUBJECT: Yes. To talk about…

DAVID: So, would you say that you're going to review that life as a mother with four children?

SUBJECT: Yes. I was patient and kind.

DAVID: And that was part of what you'd signed up for in that life?

SUBJECT: Yes.

DAVID: Well that sounds very nice. So, you were not only a good mother — did you pass those lessons of being patient and kind?

SUBJECT: Yes. [Softly] This was an easy one.

DAVID: Say that again?

SUBJECT: This was an easy one.

DAVID: I'm sorry?

SUBJECT: This was an easy life.

DAVID: Those were the easy ones, those lessons? Okay. Tell me some of the hard lessons you had signed up for in that life?

SUBJECT: There was a lot of hard work.

DAVID: [Repeating her] Lot of hard work.

SUBJECT: [Softly] I lost a lot of children…

DAVID: Say that again?

SUBJECT: I lost children, and that was hard for me.

DAVID: Those are hard lessons. Can you think of a couple more or are those the two hardest?

SUBJECT: I had a very, very simple life, and for me the hardest lesson I had to face was losing my children. I lost three.

DAVID: You lost three children?

SUBJECT: I lost one during … I don't know… childbirth or after birth? He was born alive but died soon after. I had two miscarriages.

DAVID: That is sad…eventually you had four living children, is that correct?

SUBJECT: Yes.

DAVID: So, you would have had seven children if they had all survived?

SUBJECT: Yes.

DAVID: Well, that's very sad, and that was hard losing children, wasn't it?

SUBJECT: Yes.

DAVID: Well, those are hard lessons: the pain from losing a child.

SUBJECT: But I didn't get angry and bitter.

DAVID: Good. Well, that's good. So, you didn't blame anybody for losing them, right?

SUBJECT: No.

DAVID: Were you a religious woman in that life?

SUBJECT: Yes, I studied the bible.

DAVID: Now when you went to see the wise ones, having studied the bible, did you see any angels while you were looking around?

SUBJECT: There are angels— but you don't go up to them; they come up to you. If they want to talk to you, they summon you.

DAVID: So, if they want to talk to you, they'll summon you?

SUBJECT: Yes.

DAVID: So, you just don't walk up to them and ask them questions?

SUBJECT: Yes.

DAVID: Because that's kind of rude, right?

SUBJECT: Yes.

DAVID: Or are they so advanced that it'd be like a private walking up to a general and asking him something? It's pretty structured?

SUBJECT: It's just their affairs are much more intricate than any affairs I have… I'm not that level… that advanced.

DAVID: That makes sense. So, it'd be almost like an ninth grader walking up to a PhD and asking a question… somebody else is going to handle the question besides the PhD, correct?

SUBJECT: Yes.

DAVID: That makes sense, because they've got intricate things and I'm sure they're very busy. So, you went to see your wise ones. Now tell me, what colors were your wise ones?

SUBJECT: They're purple, and there's one angel.

DAVID: So, there's an angel in the group too?

SUBJECT: Yes. Two purple and one angel. It's just my husband and I in front of this council, but I don't know his name, and I don't know why.

DAVID: You don't know whose name?

SUBJECT: I don't know his name.

DAVID: Your husband?

SUBJECT: Names…of the members of my council.

DAVID: I'm not good with names either, but that's okay. So, are there only three on your council? Two purple souls and one angel?

SUBJECT: Mhm [yes].

DAVID: Are they there to see you about that life?

SUBJECT: Mhm [yes].

DAVID: Give me an idea of what questions they asked you concerning that life?

SUBJECT: We're talking more about other lessons that I need to learn.

DAVID: And what lessons do they tell you that you need to learn?

SUBJECT: That I had an easy life.

DAVID: Even though it was a lot of hardship and work?

SUBJECT: Yes.

DAVID: They thought it was easy for you?

SUBJECT: There's other things that I need to focus on… like… I don't know what the word in my head is. [Sigh].

DAVID: So, there are other lessons they want you to learn, correct? [Pause] Adaptability? Acceptance? Forgiveness?

SUBJECT: No, I like to challenge myself. I need to have harder lessons.

DAVID: That's what they told you?

SUBJECT: Mhm [yes].

DAVID: For soul growth, right?

SUBJECT: Yes.

DAVID: And what kind of lessons? Did they give you an idea? Was it going to be like a physical or mental disability? What kind of lessons?

SUBJECT: [Pause] Physically, I'm very strong. Mentally, I'm fairly strong. It's emotional.

DAVID: More emotional situations?

SUBJECT: No, um… the word that keeps playing in my mind they're projecting to me, I don't know. I don't know what it is. It seems so far away.

DAVID: Well, as you're there with your council, how do they feel you did overall in that life?

SUBJECT: Good.

DAVID: Did you pass all the lessons?

SUBJECT: Yes, but they said that's why they're talking to me. It was an easy life, and I'm going to be challenged more next time. That's why they're talking to me. We're having a serious conversation. My husband is trying to encourage me.

DAVID: Because you're a little concerned about how hard that next life could be?

SUBJECT: No, I'm just… not responding.

DAVID: But they said you needed to take a more challenging life even though you knew you did a good job in that life. It was hard work, you lost some children, but I guess you're saying that they just didn't appreciate how well you actually did in that life with the hard work and loss, is that right?

SUBJECT: It's more… I'm meant to be more than what I am.

DAVID: So, they knew you had more ambition and drive in you to handle a harder life?

SUBJECT: Yes.

DAVID: They know that you have the ability to challenge yourself more and conquer harder assignments, is that right?

SUBJECT: And they want me to be … they want me to advance… they want me… I'm not ready to be purple; that's way out there. But I think I'm ready to do more blue soul stuff. I'm not ready to be like them, but they want me to be a leader.

DAVID: Okay, so right now what is your soul color?

SUBJECT: Green.

DAVID: You're green. With some blue?

SUBJECT: Just a little bit, but that's what we're talking about.

DAVID: Exactly. Talking about advancing up by being a leader and showing others, correct?

SUBJECT: Yes.

DAVID: That's very interesting. So, they said with some harder lives that you would evolve faster, is that correct?

SUBJECT: Yes.

DAVID: When you're there with your spirit guides, let's say the council… How many lives do they think you've had on earth? Do you see any numbers in your head?

SUBJECT: I see numbers floating around, and it's very strange.

DAVID: But it's hard to tell how many lives, correct?

SUBJECT: Yes.

DAVID: You just know you've had quite a few?

SUBJECT: Yes.

DAVID: And you feel pretty confident about that life, -------------, even though it was a hard life. Anything back in the 1800s is hard and raising kids on the farm must have been tough. But they said…you know what, you can handle harder challenges. You got paid a compliment. Your council said, "Look------------, you blew through that one, we know you can do much bigger things." Is that correct?

SUBJECT: Yes.

DAVID: There's a sense of confidence the council has in you by saying, "We believe in you. You blew through that life. We know it was easier than what you can handle." So, I can see that approach makes sense… and taking harder lives and challenges is what makes a leader, right?

SUBJECT: [Very quietly] Yes.

DAVID: Hard experiences to help others as a leader someday. So, as you're standing there, what are you looking like in front of the council?

[A "leader" doesn't necessarily mean someone who is well funded, runs and wins a political office, though they often have broad powers to decide various matters among the citizenry. True leaders lead by example and exhibit qualities such as strength and wisdom, combined with empathy and understanding and many have spiritual underpinnings, making decisions for the benefit of all. Strong examples would be Jesus, Buddha, Confucius, Mohammed, Rama, to more modern-day leaders like Mahatma Gandhi and Dr. Martin Luther King, to name a few.]

SUBJECT: Just a ball of light.

DAVID: So, you're just a ball of green energy?

SUBJECT: Mhm [yes].

DAVID: Now if you look closely, can you project a face onto your ball of green energy?

SUBJECT: I don't see faces, but I also don't feel like I look at people, if that makes sense. I feel meek.

DAVID: Okay. What color is your husband's soul?

SUBJECT: He's green.

DAVID: So, you're a pretty good match for each other?

SUBJECT: Yes.

DAVID: You guys have a lot in common, you're about the same level of evolution, and you enjoy each other. Is that right?

SUBJECT: Yes. He wasn't around much.

DAVID: He what?

SUBJECT: He wasn't around much.

DAVID: I know, you said that earlier. Let me ask you this…

SUBJECT: It was okay. He worked hard. He gave us a good life.

DAVID: So, he did pretty well with his lessons too?

SUBJECT: Yes.

DAVID: Did they think it was too easy on him as well?

SUBJECT: No, he had different lessons. To be away from us was hard.

DAVID: What kind of lessons did he have? Can you share those?

SUBJECT: No, he doesn't want to talk about them. I think that's why I'm making…

DAVID: Oh, so it's private?

SUBJECT: No, it's not that it's private; he just doesn't want to talk about it right now.

DAVID: You're sitting in front of your council, going over that life, and they said you did well, you passed your lessons. They said they want to see you do harder lessons in the future. I'm sure most councils tell that to most souls they're reviewing, because they want everyone to evolve. They want purple eventually. So, to get there, you've got to take harder stuff. So, I can see councils in most cases discussing taking harder lives with the souls they're reviewing, wanting them to challenge themselves more.

You know that's a great way to word it for councils, saying something like, "Hey, we know that life was hard, but you breezed through it.

We think that was an easier life than you could have handled. We believe in you. We see some leadership qualities. We'd like to see you handle some tougher lives for that type of soul-growth." I'm sure that's probably going on in every council meeting, because it makes sense. If you're not all the way up there, and you want to advance, you have to take harder lives, because that is the way to evolve, not only consciously but in wisdom as well.

So as your sitting in front of your council, talk to me about the angel. Do you recognize them?

SUBJECT: No.

DAVID: Okay.

SUBJECT: He's very quiet.

DAVID: Who seems to be leading the group?

SUBJECT: There's... the two purple...

DAVID: Who's the council person in control? Is there someone in charge?

SUBJECT: Yes, and the purple soul who is leading this council meeting is talking to the other purple soul who is kind of their assistant. But not everyone speaks... only the one head person talks to me. They talk to each other, and then the three of them talk amongst themselves, but only one person speaks directly to me.

DAVID: And do they feel pretty powerful?

SUBJECT: Yes.

DAVID: Because they're advanced beings. You know these beings have done a lot of hard stuff and have had a lot of challenging lives and experiences to evolve to purple souls, is that right?

SUBJECT: Mhm [yes].

DAVID: So, let's say the council meeting is over. They're happy with you. Now after you leave your council meeting, where do you go next?

SUBJECT: [Mumbled] To visit other people in my group.

DAVID: Say that again.

SUBJECT: To visit other people in my group.

DAVID: So, you're going to visit with them?

SUBJECT: I'm going to see my friends.

DAVID: Are they glad to see you back?

SUBJECT: Yes.

DAVID: Did you miss them?

SUBJECT: I did.

DAVID: So, they're a fun bunch you hang out with?

SUBJECT: We just talk. We discuss. We share experiences. It's not… I don't know how to explain it…

DAVID: It's not like you're going to hang out and just have fun?

SUBJECT: No.

DAVID: So, it's a more serious discussion?

SUBJECT: We're in the hallway with the doors again.

[The subject had mentioned she was in the "hallway with doors" earlier in the regression when asked what she saw. When I probed if she had passed on, she replied no. In reviewing, I feel strongly that she had already died and was on the other side, but the experience felt so real she mistook the heavenly realm (the hallway with doors) as her past life.]

DAVID: Do you have something like dorms? Where do you live?

SUBJECT: It's not really a building; it's a space, a vast space that everybody is in.

DAVID: So, you have this vast space, and souls are all throughout it?

SUBJECT: Mhm [yes].

DAVID: You can blink your eyes to the very end and it's just infinite, is that right?

SUBJECT: As soon as you feel like you're at the end, it continues to go.

DAVID: Do any of the souls live in a little place they built, maybe something similar to what they had on earth to make them feel better? Do they ever build any gardens or familiar rooms or houses?

SUBJECT: Yes, but I'm not there.

DAVID: What do you mean, you're "not there?"

SUBJECT: That's somewhere else.

DAVID: That's somewhere else. Are there different places you can go as a soul?

SUBJECT: It's just not the area I'm in right now.

DAVID: So, this is where you go to see friends and hang out, but nothing you've created is here, right?

SUBJECT: No creating, we're just sharing our experiences of past lives, things that went on.

DAVID: Does it feel good to share?

SUBJECT: It does.

DAVID: Because it kind of brings you back to home more, doesn't it?

SUBJECT: It makes me excited to hear their happiness and their enthusiasm.

DAVID: Have some of those souls… are they all green mostly?

SUBJECT: Mhm [yes].

DAVID: Did some of them have some pretty hard lives that they talked about?

SUBJECT: Mhm [yes].

DAVID: So, you're all comparing notes. Do all of you have different councils, or the same council?

SUBJECT: Different.

DAVID: So, everybody has pretty much a different council. So, there aren't too many souls who have the same council?

SUBJECT: A couple of them have the same as me, but no.

DAVID: But not a lot, is that correct?

SUBJECT: Yes, that's correct.

DAVID: Well, that's interesting. Now are most of the councils just a couple of members or does it vary?

SUBJECT: It's always three on mine.

DAVID: Does your husband have more than three?

SUBJECT: No, he has the same council.

DAVID: So, his council is the same as yours?

SUBJECT: Yes.

DAVID: Okay...

SUBJECT: That's why he came with me.

DAVID: I understand. A good support too, right?

SUBJECT: Yes.

DAVID: So, you're seeing the purple souls, the wise ones. Now what's the evolution of a purple soul? A deep purple soul, do you know?

[Though I knew the soul evolution colors, I wanted to see what the subject's interpretation was as she had no idea of soul color evolution prior to her hypnotic induction. It was not until tapping deep into her super-consciousness and into the other side that this previously unknown information was readily forthcoming for her.]

SUBJECT: Purple is the highest here other than angels.

DAVID: So, dark purple is the highest state of evolution, and above that are the angels. Now what about ascended masters like Jesus for example? When you think of him in your mind, what color is his aura or his soul?

SUBJECT: [Mumbles]

DAVID: Say that again?

SUBJECT: I've never met him.

DAVID: You never met him, okay. Did you ever meet any disciples?

SUBJECT: No.

DAVID: But you see some angels where we are now, is that correct?

SUBJECT: Yes.

DAVID: Anyway, let's stay where you are now. We just spoke to your council. They're happy with that life. And you're standing there, looking around viewing all these different souls with all their different colors. Do you see any other angels around?

SUBJECT: Just the one that's on my council.

DAVID: Just the one on your council. Can we go and talk to them for a minute? Would that be okay?

SUBJECT: He's talking to the wise ones.

DAVID: Good. Well anyway, when available, I wanted to ask if it's okay, looking at the life you're in currently, what would they want to tell us about you? What skills have you brought into this life beyond compassion and loving children and things like that? Things that you are not yet aware of. And I'd like to ask if there's anything they can tell us about your stomach beyond what we did tonight, as far as healing. And let's see if they say anything about your health, and what they suggest. And in this life, what is it going to take to move you forward? Can I ask those questions?

SUBJECT: Yes.

DAVID: Okay. So those are the questions.

SUBJECT: [Mumbles]

DAVID: What? Say that again?

SUBJECT: Strong will. I have a strong will. And I have to fight through my struggles and that's what causes the stomach issues. I keep it all inside, and I think about it too much.

DAVID: That sounds like great advice.

SUBJECT: I have to let my will overcome it and not give in to other thoughts, no matter how difficult it gets.

DAVID: Very good information, and I think dead-on. I mean, that's beautifully said.

SUBJECT: And they're laughing.

DAVID: Say that again?

SUBJECT: They're laughing.

DAVID: Why are they laughing?

SUBJECT: As they humbly know their information is good, it's a collective effort with my best intents in mind.

DAVID: No doubt. I'm very impressed. That kind of nailed it, I think. And I guess the other question would be, if we get rid of the stress, anxiety in the stomach…

SUBJECT: Patience.

DAVID: Is that for you to have more patience?

SUBJECT: With myself.

DAVID: Yes. Any other good tips?

SUBJECT: We were just talking about… I felt very meek when we were talking before to them, and when they started talking about other things, I became very … down is not the word… I went from a blob to a more formed being, if that makes sense.

DAVID: Okay.

SUBJECT: I don't know, as soon as we started talking about it, it was like I was no longer meek, and that's something I needed to learn, but it wasn't in this life.

DAVID: Okay.

SUBJECT: It was in another life.

DAVID: They're well aware of the things you and I have done as far as healing, and for your stomach, among other things. And it almost feels to me like a temporary, hypnotic band aid, on the issues. What else can she do to keep the pain from coming back?

SUBJECT: They said I need to meditate more. I need to be in my head more.

DAVID: So, meditate more?

SUBJECT: Just do more of those.

DAVID: That's what they're suggesting?

SUBJECT: Yes.

DAVID: Do they think the healing recordings help?

SUBJECT: Yes. I need to stay awake longer.

DAVID: Say that again?

SUBJECT: I need to stay focused longer or awake longer.

DAVID: Awake longer, during these sessions?

SUBJECT: Mhm [yes].

DAVID: So, looking at this life, is there anything else I can help her with? Is there anything else, when using hypnosis, that I can do for her as far as her physical or mental health? Anything I can add to these sessions? Or, just more or less, trying to get her to stay awake longer?

SUBJECT: Baby steps.

DAVID: Baby steps, okay. Could we ask them this?

SUBJECT: No, that's what they said. It's part of the lesson for me. I have to learn to listen to myself more.

DAVID: Well, that's right. I think that information they gave you originally on the…

SUBJECT: They say that I'm very wise, but I act before thinking. Impulsive.

DAVID: Well, can I ask the council, just out of the blue…

SUBJECT: [interjects] Joseph, but I don't know which one of the purple souls is Joseph. That's… Joseph [pronounced "Ho-sef]. That's what they keep saying. That's Joseph, right?

DAVID: Oh, Joseph, that's his name?

SUBJECT: Yes.

DAVID: Thank you.

SUBJECT: But it's the other blue one that wasn't talking… or purple, I mean, the wise-one.

DAVID: Is the person who does the most talking named Joseph?

SUBJECT: No.

DAVID: It's the other one?

SUBJECT: Yeah, Joseph told me… "Just tell him Joseph, Joseph."

DAVID: Because that's… yeah, I understand. Well, I want to thank your council, ----------, for all this information. Do they have any parting words for ------------?

SUBJECT: [Long pause] No, I said thank you and they kind of just went away.

DAVID: All right. Well, thank you very much, council. I'm glad you gave me the honor and privilege of coming to her council meeting. Thank you. So, I want you to begin to see where you go next from here. Where do you create things?

SUBJECT: That's where I'm going. It slowly begins to look more like earth.

DAVID: It slowly begins to look more like earth, okay.

SUBJECT: There are defined-areas, defined-objects.

DAVID: How much like earth, or how different?

SUBJECT: It's land. It seems very flat. It's very vast, but very flat. And it could be anything you want it to be.

DAVID: Now do you have certain ground you build on, or do you just work where you want to?

SUBJECT: Each group kind of has their own area, and groups stay together.

DAVID: And groups stay together. Now describe some of the structures that your group built or likes to visit, and describe the one that you like to go to that you've created.

SUBJECT: I like the ocean.

DAVID: Say that again.

SUBJECT: I like the water, the ocean.

DAVID: You like the ocean. Did you build some ocean for yourself?

SUBJECT: I built a waterfall with rocks.

DAVID: Wow, sounds pretty.

SUBJECT: And grass.

DAVID: Now do you sit on the edge of the waterfall?

SUBJECT: Yes.

DAVID: Do you have a little house or structure you go into that you created?

SUBJECT: Just a little cottage. It's very…

DAVID: And it's near the waterfall?

SUBJECT: Mhm, yes.

DAVID: That must be pretty. Pretty relaxing, isn't it?

SUBJECT: It's where I go when I want to be alone. I enjoy being with everybody, but I enjoy being by myself sometimes.

DAVID: So, this is your little place to get away?

SUBJECT: It's not away from everything but yes, it's …

DAVID: So, you have more privacy here?

SUBJECT: Anybody can come into it, but nobody does. It's like you're in your own little …

DAVID: World.

SUBJECT: Yes.

DAVID: Or little scene. That sounds really pretty and nice. Are there trees and other plants there?

SUBJECT: Mhm, yes.

DAVID: Do you have a hammock?

SUBJECT: I have a fishing pole.

DAVID: You've got a fishing pole. Do you fish?

SUBJECT: I'm wearing overalls, which is funny because I have a human form. That's why I said it's almost like earth, but it's not earth. And you're in human form, but you're not human.

DAVID: That's interesting. What does your body look like compared to earth form?

SUBJECT: The same. I'm a woman. It's just like this area, like I'm in my own head with a memory. But it's the happy place I built.

DAVID: So anyway, this sounds very interesting. Describe some of your closer friends in the group and what they built. Give me some ideas.

SUBJECT: There are gardens.

DAVID: So, you see some gardens, are they pretty?

SUBJECT: Yes.

DAVID: Do you see any big caves or cool houses?

SUBJECT: There are cool buildings that are pretty.

DAVID: And do these souls take the whole building?

SUBJECT: Mhm, yes.

DAVID: Well, that's something. You sound like you have the best nature thing. Does anybody have more of a nature-type environment?

SUBJECT: Everybody has a little bit of nature in their areas. It's more nature here than there is structure.

DAVID: And that's in most cases?

SUBJECT: With my group.

DAVID: Now does your group get together to play games, ever? Do you do any fun stuff at night?

SUBJECT: We invite each other into our places, and it's like a party here on earth but doing whatever you want to do. So, if one of my soul-friends enjoys gardening, I'll go garden with her for a period of time and help her build her garden and plant things.

DAVID: That sounds great. Now do you ever jump in your waterfall?

SUBJECT: Yes.

DAVID: Do you have a pond at the bottom of it?

SUBJECT: It's a river.

DAVID: So, you have a river, wow. And that's why you went fishing, because the river just keeps on going, huh?

SUBJECT: Mhm [yes].

DAVID: Did you ever go to the end of the river?

SUBJECT: Uh-uh [no].

DAVID: That's something you might want to try sometime. Walk along the banks and keep extending it in your mind farther and farther, and pretty soon maybe you'll want to follow to the end of that river to see whether it flows into an ocean and if there's maybe an island out in it. Don't be afraid to expand your boundaries to what you're allowed to do. Okay?

SUBJECT: Why do I feel afraid? Not afraid. Meek? Why do I feel … I don't know how else to explain it. These thoughts that go through, it makes me feel like I shouldn't be doing that.

DAVID: Like you shouldn't be doing what?

SUBJECT: Going to the end of the river.

DAVID: Creativity is important and especially where you are now… In other words, don't be afraid to expand it with your mind. You've got a nice waterfall and cottage. Do you have flowers planted around your cottage?

SUBJECT: Mhm [yes].

DAVID: So, you have a pretty nice setup already. Well you could change things a little bit too. You could throw in a hammock maybe or do whatever you want to do, perhaps another tree. Go walk on top of the waterfall. Did you ever go to the top of it?

SUBJECT: No, there's a big rock, and I always sit on the big rock.

DAVID: Is it at the top or the bottom?

SUBJECT: It's by the waterfall.

DAVID: Right. Now let me ask you this: Have you ever gone to the top of the waterfall?

SUBJECT: I can, but I don't.

DAVID: Are you nervous to?

SUBJECT: No.

DAVID: Okay.

SUBJECT: I just like my rock.

DAVID: That's fine. So, it's very restful, isn't it? It sounds very nice.

SUBJECT: I'm very at peace. I don't feel bad… when I felt meek, like nervous, I don't know… like I don't know if I'm supposed to be doing that, when you said certain things.

DAVID: Yes.

SUBJECT: And when we were talking to the wise ones, I didn't look at them because I felt like I shouldn't do that. It was almost like I should be looking down.

DAVID: [Chuckle] So, you felt a little nervous, huh?

SUBJECT: Yeah.

DAVID: Well, let me tell you, it's okay for me to come to your council meetings occasionally. I won't go to all of them, but I think in this case, you know, they knew me, they were laughing and having a good time too.

SUBJECT: Yes.

DAVID: The main thing is that they know you had a good life, and they know you're here, and they know I'm here to help you, no doubt. They know I do this type of thing and when we asked questions about you, look at the very good remarks they shared with you. Later, you want to go back and review what was covered and learn from that.

So, when you say, "meek," you know, Jesus said, "The meek will inherit the earth," right? So, you can be meek to some degree, as long as somebody's not trying to hurt you or your family. If someone's in danger and you're trying to assist them, don't be meek then. But you want to be able to expand too. You want to be able to open your mind until you see in 360 degrees, where you see all around you. And by starting to do that, you're going to advance more. Okay?

SUBJECT: Yes.

DAVID: So, here's the thing with creativity: When I asked initially what I could create, I was a little nervous at first, like, "Gosh, can I really build past this area?" I thought, "It looks all dark over there. I don't know if I'm supposed to." So, you're going to feel that nervousness initially, like I did. And then I think you'll find that, no, they want you to be able to expand, because it's in your consciousness. So, then you just say, "Stop me if I'm not allowed to."

Don't be afraid to walk up to the top of the waterfall or trace that river further downstream. As you proceed farther and farther up above the waterfall, maybe someday you'll want to do something like put a nice, big Indian tent from an Indian past life you may have had and a fireplace at the top. Perhaps sit in front of a nice fire and maybe you'll want to stay there for a while. Don't be afraid to go beyond what you've already created. You love your rock, but work to expand beyond that, okay? In other words, don't be timid about having other areas you'd like to go to.

Because it's like here on earth to some degree. We expand if we want to expand. We build not only for ourselves, but for others as well... and through life we often expand our world. But we don't have to. We can just get through life and scurry out and back home again. Always remember and say to yourself: "I'm an immortal, powerful soul. I'm here for experiences. I'm going to try and meditate more, because that's what my council is telling me, which is a good idea." By meditating, it will help you see your path clearer.

I would look to find what's going to make your life easier and make the "Law of Attraction," work for you. And when negative people are around and when needed, think to yourself, "I'm going to have on my golden suit of protection, and I'm going to wear this thing. I'm going to portray to others this beautiful golden light radiating off of me." And like-minded people are going to say, "Wow, that girl has positive energy. She didn't say anything to me, but I can tell she's very positive. I feel her energy." That's how you attract things. Negative energy is going to run from that. They don't know what they're doing, which is fine. All will find their way someday.

But you have things to do now in this life. So, you've got to watch getting bogged down in negativity. If you feel it coming at you, like an energy vampire getting ready to suck the energy out of you, whether it's your sister-in-law you described, difficult ex-husband, or anybody else — BANG! — Put on that golden suit. Nothing is going to go through that. That is divine light, and it's immortal. Through this reading tonight, sitting in front of your council, now you should know how divine things are, right? How immortal you are. This is real. This is how it works.

So, here we are after meeting your council. So now, when this session is over as you go on through life, and as you step your feet back down on earth, back to earth school, don't let your feet get bogged down. Keep moving, right? And if you feel something negative coming at you, then call on protection, call on Archangel Michael, and get his wings around you. Put that golden suit on and walk through life confident and powerful, because this life is going to be over some day.

So, talking about what you said about meekness, think about this. Say to yourself, "Look, what am I fearful of? What am I scared of? Is this an illusion messing with my head?" It's almost like looking at life through a virtual reality headset, because that's basically what it is like to a degree. Your consciousness and mind are housed in an infinitely amazing bio-suit to experience life, lessons and experiences here. If you look at life in this way, the suit comes off at death, and back to the "real" reality. It's game over for that life, and you're going to know that your soul will always be around.

And say to yourself: "If I have negative people bouncing toward me, I'm going to repel them back with positive energy, and I'm going to go on and do my thing." It is like living in a virtual reality world here playing the game, and as others wake up from the cosmic amnesia that surrounds most, they can work toward finding out why they're here.

We can look at our individual reasons for incarnating, but we will never have all the answers concerning the life lessons we chose before incarnating. None of us are ever really going to know what our lessons are in every life we have, and that's what makes it hard. You will never really know what you're here to learn. Meditation and past-life regressions can get you closer to understanding your purpose here. The easiest way to determine whether a life lesson has come into your path is if the situation is challenging or has negative implications that you must learn to overcome. It is possible to get a good idea when you're facing lessons you agreed to undertake before you incarnated when you are forced to persevere and rise up above what you considered your limitations. How you react to tragedy and traumatic events is what matters.

As Buddha said, "How someone acts toward you is their karma, how you respond is yours." Figure that could be a lesson in some form or fashion coming at you and try to react in a way positively beneficial for all parties. Easier said than done, but that's what makes the challenge or lesson you signed up for voluntarily before incarnating a strong test that adds to soul growth when you pass.

Try to go with the flow and if negativity comes your way, say to yourself, "You know, they're just not awake. They're stressed, they're caught in earth school, and can't get beyond their hurts, their traumas and are projecting." Maybe there are things holding them back, and they're throwing negative energy at you out of frustration. That's the kind of stuff you want to stay away from, okay? Just block it out. Put on your golden suit. Don't let negative energy get to your heart again, and it won't work its way toward your stomach, causing you additional pain beyond the IBS. Just get away from it. Shoo it out. Listen to this recording later, which will help you figure out how to keep negative energy from affecting you.

Don't be afraid to carry an amethyst or another protective crystal in your pocket. Crystals are very, very powerful. Amethyst and other crystals have power, and they'll protect you. People have been using crystals for eons, thousands and thousands of years. I'm sure you've been around crystals in your life and other lives you may have had.

You know, it's good to keep some protection around you and say a prayer of protection. Call on the angels around you. Say to your spirit guides, "Hey, spirit guides, I'm feeling a little nervous here now. Help me fight through this. Help me feel the strength and the power coming in." And at the same time, visualize that golden light coming into you right through your crown chakra.

I think you'll be amazed when you approach different things down the line using this technique. You're going to feel that sense of calmness or peace. You're thinking about negative things too much and getting bogged down on a wheel of negativity. When feeling anxious or down, if you just repeat to yourself, "Heck with it, I'm not wasting more time on negative things, and I'm going to do something positive. I'm going to set some goals." You might clean the house, make something to eat that's special, take a class, wow them at work, or help others in your community, but you're not going to entertain negativity. That's how you want to approach negative people who come at you. Say to yourself, "What are they dreaming that their negativity can get to me?"

Block them off, and don't respond to negative texts and calls. Educate others where you can. Try to gauge a person's growth, where their mind is, what they believe in, and kind of add little things where you can here and there to their knowledge or understanding.

If you're quoting things from science, you'll have a better shot sharing with others. Things like, "This meditation thing must work; these scientists at Harvard are doing mind-studies and look how well the ones participating are doing." So, you want to kind of educate as you go through life.

So, as you relax, you shared with us that nice creation you made, and did your Council give you an idea when you may come back to earth again after that life? Or do you have no idea?

SUBJECT: Right after.

DAVID: So literally you're going to come back pretty darn soon.

SUBJECT: Mhm [yes].

DAVID: So, they aren't going to let you hang out in heaven too long, right?

SUBJECT: Uh-uh [no]. I have things to work on.

DAVID: How's your pain now?

SUBJECT: All gone.

DAVID: Glad to hear.

~

Hard Life and a Council Pleased

The hypnotic induction in this case was left out, as it mirrored previous ones used to hypnotically regress clients. This client is a female in her early thirties. Join us on her journey as she recounts her death in a past life and meets her soul council on the other side.

DAVID: [End of hypnotic induction] Now as we go drifting along, what hard lessons did you experience in this past-life?

SUBJECT: There was a fire.

DAVID: There was a what?

SUBJECT: Fire. [Quietly] My house burned down.

DAVID: Say that again?

SUBJECT: My house burned down.

DAVID: Your house burned down. That's a hard lesson. And what other hard lessons did you have in that life?

SUBJECT: [Long pause] Treachery.

DAVID: There was some treachery involved?

SUBJECT: Yes.

DAVID: Okay.

SUBJECT: [Very quietly] A lot of…

DAVID: Say that again.

SUBJECT: A lot of death. A lot of killing.

DAVID: A lot of killing and death. That's certainly not good.

SUBJECT: I was helping.

DAVID: Again?

SUBJECT: I was taking care of the wounded.

DAVID: You were taking care of the wounded?

SUBJECT: Mhm [yes].

DAVID: Were you at a battle?

SUBJECT: Yes, we were fighting with our neighbors, with the other people.

DAVID: So, it was two families fighting against each other?

SUBJECT: [Mumble] Not biological families.

DAVID: Not biological families. Now does this have anything to do with the Civil War?

SUBJECT: Not yet.

DAVID: So, it was before the Civil War?

SUBJECT: Yes.

DAVID: But you're having big battles with your neighbors. Is it over land or what's it over?

SUBJECT: Land.

DAVID: So, land mostly?

SUBJECT: And livestock.

DAVID: And livestock. That was a hard life. Tell me more about that life. Were you a man or a woman?

SUBJECT: A woman.

DAVID: And your house burned down.

SUBJECT: [Mumbled] They set it on fire. The people we were fighting with.

DAVID: Oh, the people you were fighting with set it on fire. Okay. Now were you married?

SUBJECT: Yes. I had children. There were lots of children staying with me when the house burned down.

DAVID: Did they get out in time?

SUBJECT: They came out in time.

DAVID: Did you get out?

SUBJECT: Yes.

DAVID: So, you made it out of the house? Now, where did it feel like you were located? What territory do you think?

SUBJECT: Midwest.

DAVID: Somewhere in the Midwest? Did you have any mountains around you or was it pretty flat?

SUBJECT: It was flat. There wasn't a lot of population around.

DAVID: And what other lessons did you take on in that life that were difficult?

SUBJECT: [Pause] I had to learn to endure.

DAVID: You had to what?

SUBJECT: Endure.

DAVID: You had to endure.

SUBJECT: Endure pain. Endure… I had to learn to put others first.

DAVID: Wow, that's a hard lesson.

SUBJECT: And to put my pain, my suffering away, because other people were suffering worse.

DAVID: Was that because of the killing and shooting?

SUBJECT: Because of everything. I was in a better position than most. Most of the people that were with me were very poor, and I was not as poor as them.

DAVID: So, it made it very difficult for them to eat and everything else, didn't it?

SUBJECT: Yes.

DAVID: Did you help them with meals when they didn't have anything?

SUBJECT: They lived on my land.

DAVID: Did you have cows?

SUBJECT: I had everything.

DAVID: So, you had a lot of livestock?

SUBJECT: Mhm [yes].

DAVID: And how many acres do you think you had?

SUBJECT: As many as I wanted.

DAVID: Now as you see yourself in that life, and you see everything getting older and older…

SUBJECT: I'm not that old when I die.

DAVID: Oh, how old were you?

SUBJECT: I was young. I was in my late forties.

DAVID: In your forties. And what did you die from, do you remember?

SUBJECT: I was sick, and I just died.

DAVID: So, you aren't sure what it was, but you got sick and died, is that right?

SUBJECT: Yes.

DAVID: Did you die in bed with a fever while very sick?

SUBJECT: I died trying to help others.

DAVID: So, you died trying to help some of the…

SUBJECT: I was sick, and I was trying to help others. And I was just falling, like, trying to take care of all of the other people that were sick. We all were sick. It's…

DAVID: And you weren't sure what everybody was sick from, huh?

SUBJECT: No.

DAVID: Was it from some bad flu sweeping through, maybe?

SUBJECT: Mhm [yes].

DAVID: Did a lot of people die from it?

SUBJECT: Mhm [yes].

DAVID: And this was before the Civil War, is that correct?

SUBJECT: Mhm [yes].

DAVID: Do you think it may have been 1820s or 30s or 40s or what decade or year?

SUBJECT: I don't know.

DAVID: Sometime before the Civil War though?

SUBJECT: Mhm [yes].

DAVID: So, people are getting sick. And you are in your forties, you're sick too, and you're just hustling along, dying basically. And then you just fell over and died, I guess, huh?

SUBJECT: Mhm [yes].

DAVID: Now when you fell over and saw your death, did you see yourself as a spirit staring at your dead body?

SUBJECT: Yes.

DAVID: And how long did you stand there?

SUBJECT: A long time.

DAVID: A long time? Were you hoping that you got back up? Did you try to get the body back up?

SUBJECT: I tried to get the body back up. Everybody else was so sick.

DAVID: Did you see other ghosts standing around that had just died too?

SUBJECT: Yes, a lot of them ran.

DAVID: They what?

SUBJECT: They just went. They just disappeared fast.

DAVID: So, you stayed, but a lot of them who you saw die had come out of their bodies and then just disappeared?

SUBJECT: Yes.

DAVID: Is that correct?

SUBJECT: Yes.

DAVID: Was that pretty much like, "Wow, what's going on here"? Did you know you were dead?

SUBJECT: Yes.

DAVID: So, you knew you were dead, but you didn't want to leave, because you were still concerned about sick people, I guess?

SUBJECT: I fought to stay as long as I could.

DAVID: Because… why?

SUBJECT: Because they needed me.

DAVID: Because you knew the people there needed you, is that right?

SUBJECT: Yes.

DAVID: That's really touching. So, you felt they needed you there. You tried to stay as long as possible.

SUBJECT: I need… [mumbles].

DAVID: Say that again please?

SUBJECT: I need to be needed.

DAVID: One more time?

SUBJECT: I need to be needed. I liked it.

DAVID: Okay, you like what you're doing right?

SUBJECT: Yes.

DAVID: Who eventually came for you?

SUBJECT: The children and I went.

DAVID: Say that again?

SUBJECT: The children and I went.

DAVID: The children?

SUBJECT: Mhm [yes].

DAVID: Your children or other children?

SUBJECT: I waited for all the children that were staying at my house. We all went together.

DAVID: Did they all die?

SUBJECT: We all died.

DAVID: Did any die in the fire?

SUBJECT: No, we all were very sick, everyone that was with me in that room. There was not that many people that were my age, but there was young children, as young as five or six, and I waited for them, because I knew they were all going to be coming with me.

DAVID: Because they had gotten sick and died?

SUBJECT: Because they were all sick too. And they had not passed before me; they passed shortly after.

DAVID: So, a lot of people were passing away, is that correct?

SUBJECT: Yes, both sides. Very few people lived.

DAVID: So, people were passing away. You were in the Midwest.

SUBJECT: Mhm [yes].

DAVID: Did it feel like a bad flu? A virus?

SUBJECT: A fever.

DAVID: It was a high fever?

SUBJECT: Yes. And hallucinations.

DAVID: And how did your body feel?

SUBJECT: I had a rash. I was freezing cold and then burning hot. I couldn't stop sweating. And weak.

DAVID: That must have been terrible.

SUBJECT: And I was trying to take care of everybody. I kept falling.

DAVID: That was a hard life, wasn't it?

SUBJECT: Yes.

DAVID: When you passed away, who came for you eventually to take you somewhere?

SUBJECT: The children and I all just went together.

DAVID: Oh, that's right, you said that. So, you waited for the children. Did you all go back somewhere together?

SUBJECT: Yes, we all went to the other side together.

DAVID: So, you all went to the other side together, okay. And when you arrived on the other side, what did you see?

SUBJECT: My family.

DAVID: You saw your family.

SUBJECT: My group.

DAVID: Say that again?

SUBJECT: My group was waiting for me.

DAVID: And your group was there.

SUBJECT: All of them.

DAVID: Everyone in your group? Well that's a nice welcoming, isn't it?

SUBJECT: Mhm [yes].

DAVID: Were you pretty happy that they all came?

SUBJECT: Mhm [yes].

DAVID: It was pretty nice, wasn't it?

SUBJECT: Mhm [yes].

DAVID: So, you saw your group. Now did you have any spirit guides coming up to you?

SUBJECT: Yes.

DAVID: And what are they saying?

SUBJECT: [Pause] I feel like I'm getting approval.

DAVID: Good, so you—

SUBJECT: It's not time. It's not time for us to talk. But I feel like I'm getting approval.

DAVID: Approval for that life?

SUBJECT: Like I did a good job.

DAVID: Yes. I would say you did. I'm impressed. And that was one of the harder lives you needed to do, right?

SUBJECT: Mhm [yes].

DAVID: And you did well in this one, didn't you?

SUBJECT: Mhm [yes].

DAVID: So, they were pretty happy and saying, "Wow, this soul took those challenges and worked them." Is that right?

SUBJECT: Mhm [yes].

DAVID: So, you felt pretty good about yourself too, didn't you?

SUBJECT: Mhm [yes].

DAVID: Because it was hard, very hard, right?

SUBJECT: Mhm [yes].

DAVID: Do you think looking back at your other lives, that this life with the sickness and the killings, the pain and the hard work and everything…

SUBJECT: That was the hardest one I had.

DAVID: That was the hardest life you've ever had? Is that correct?

SUBJECT: Up to that point, yes. I had harder lives after.

DAVID: So, you had harder lives after that life. Okay.

SUBJECT: But that life, that was only a few lives ago. And that was a hard life.

DAVID: That 1850 or whatever life?

SUBJECT: Mhm [yes].

DAVID: And that life you're telling me was only a few lives ago?

SUBJECT: I've only had a couple of different earth experiences since.

DAVID: So, between that life, where you died in your forties of illness, to this life you're in now, how many lives were in between those?

SUBJECT: Four.

DAVID: So, you had four other lives including this one, since that life, is that correct?

SUBJECT: Mhm [yes].

DAVID: Now out of those four, looking at those, which one was the hardest, do you think?

SUBJECT: [Long pause]

DAVID: Any of them stand out?

SUBJECT: This life is very difficult for me.

DAVID: This life has been a hard life for you?

SUBJECT: And two lives ago.

DAVID: So, this life's hard and two lives ago. And what was that life?

SUBJECT: But I don't talk about it. I didn't do a very good job.

DAVID: Okay, but it was a harder life, you think?

SUBJECT: Mhm [yes].

DAVID: But you don't like to talk about it?

SUBJECT: Uh-uh [no]. I don't want to remember it.

DAVID: But you grew from those experiences though, didn't you? You learned something, right?

SUBJECT: Yes.

DAVID: Well, that's what it's all about. Some lives will not be fun. It's like, "This difficult life left an imprint on me." But we know it's just…

SUBJECT: There's a lot of red when I talk about it.

DAVID: There's a lot of what?

SUBJECT: Red.

DAVID: A lot of red?

SUBJECT: Mhm [yes].

DAVID: Do you feel scared to talk about it?

SUBJECT: I feel not happy to talk about it.

DAVID: You feel what?

SUBJECT: Not happy.

DAVID: Not happy, okay. Do you feel it's something you someday might just want to release so you don't feel that way about it anymore? In other words, you realize that it's just a life?

SUBJECT: Yes.

DAVID: And it shouldn't affect us that much, right?

SUBJECT: Yes.

DAVID: So, this life, you feel is hard though, right? Let me ask you this, going back to that life where you keeled over in your forties, and then you stayed there and eventually the children came and you went with them to the other side, was that what you called heaven, right?

SUBJECT: Mhm [yes].

DAVID: Now, your spirit guide came up to you, and you were happy, and you received approval for the success you achieved in that life.

SUBJECT: Mhm [yes].

DAVID: They were proud of you in that life. So, we go from there. Is he taking you to your council meeting or when do you go to that?

SUBJECT: Not yet.

DAVID: I want you to go to that time as you're enjoying yourself. And as you're relaxing, we're counting down to relax you more. We're going to now approach, in that life, the council. Let's see what they say about you taking harder challenges. So, as you're standing there, all of the sudden we're at your council meeting.

DAVID: And how many council members are there?

SUBJECT: I don't know. There are a lot of people.

DAVID: So, they're all here to listen in on this council meeting?

SUBJECT: I don't know.

DAVID: Are your spirit guides with you?

SUBJECT: They're here, but they're not with me.

DAVID: They're not with you. So, you're sitting there and all of a sudden you look up and how many wise ones are there?

SUBJECT: [Mumbled] There's five wise ones.

DAVID: Say that again?

SUBJECT: There are five wise ones.

DAVID: So, you have five wise ones and you have an angel?

SUBJECT: No Angel.

DAVID: Any blue souls?

SUBJECT: All purple.

DAVID: They're all purple?

SUBJECT: Mhm [yes].

DAVID: All five?

SUBJECT: Mhm [yes].

DAVID: So that's going to be the council for this life is that right?

SUBJECT: Mhm [yes].

DAVID: Now are any of these purple ones… have you ever seen them on other councils for you?

SUBJECT: There are two that are on all my councils. Two of them are always with me.

DAVID: And three new ones?

SUBJECT: Yes.

DAVID: Well, overall, how do they think you did in this life?

SUBJECT: I did good.

DAVID: Were they proud of you?

SUBJECT: Yes.

DAVID: Were they impressed that you took on what, in their eyes, were extra challenges? A harder life?

SUBJECT: Yes.

DAVID: So, they were pleased to see you do well with that life and try to help others, right?

SUBJECT: Yes.

DAVID: Are there any lessons they think you needed to pass that you didn't pass in that life? How did you make out on the lessons you signed up for?

SUBJECT: I didn't… Some of the lessons I didn't master. I did a very good job, but I didn't master.

DAVID: Okay.

SUBJECT: And they want me to master them.

DAVID: I understand. And give us an idea what some of those lessons might have been?

SUBJECT: [Long pause] Self-compassion.

DAVID: Self-compassion, okay.

SUBJECT: Always self-compassion.

DAVID: And what else?

SUBJECT: [Long pause]

DAVID: Anything else?

SUBJECT: I have… [Pause] I'm very good at keeping it together.

DAVID: So, in that life or this life they thought you did a good job of keeping things together?

SUBJECT: That life.

DAVID: It sounds like you did. So, they were pretty proud overall, is that right?

SUBJECT: Yes.

DAVID: So, they liked that you did very well on some of the lessons, but a few you didn't quite master, and they want you to do a little extra down the line on those you didn't pass in new lives, is that right?

SUBJECT: Yes.

DAVID: And did they say anything about you still needing to take harder and harder challenges?

SUBJECT: Yes.

DAVID: So, they want to keep pushing you because they think you could do even harder lives, is that right?

SUBJECT: But I don't want to.

DAVID: [Chuckle] Because lives are hard, is that right?

SUBJECT: I didn't do so good in one life, and I don't want to repeat my mistakes and not do so good again.

DAVID: You didn't do so well in that red life, or whatever?

SUBJECT: Mhm [yes]. I see red when I think about it.

DAVID: Well, some day you might want to bring in your spirit guides and council and ask something like this, "With gratitude, I would like the council and my spirit guides to review that life I had difficulty in with me again. It's still bothering me, and I want to do better next time when facing similar challenges." And they'll do that for you. And next time around you'll put those lessons you didn't do so well on behind you in another life. And you will move forward. I can understand if that life where you didn't do so well is in your recent past, and you remember it as you do now, it can affect you negatively.

SUBJECT: Yes. I felt like I took on too much in that life.

DAVID: Do you think they loaded up your plate a little too high?

SUBJECT: I think I loaded up my plate too high.

DAVID: And on the other side it is easier to say, "Yeah, yeah, add that to the list, why not?" It's easier to do that on the other side, and when you get down here to earth school and have cosmic amnesia, not knowing why you're here, it's a whole different world.

SUBJECT: Yes.

DAVID: In other words, up there it's like…

SUBJECT: "Yeah, sure, okay, whatever…"

DAVID: Something like, "Okay, sure, add that, it's not going to be easy, it's another hard course, but I'll get through it." And then you come down and it's a wake-up call, isn't it?

SUBJECT: Yes.

DAVID: So, it's tough. Well, it sounds like you did well in that life, so they were happy. So overall the council was five members. Does the Council see ------------ finding her path through deeper meditations? Finding more peace and less anxiety? Do they see that for her?

SUBJECT: She takes on other people's emotions.

DAVID: So, she needs to stop that to a good degree, is that right?

SUBJECT: She needs to use the layers of protection she's taught.

DAVID: Do they think that maybe I'm helping her with that on a simple level?

SUBJECT: One council member said, "You know you are."

DAVID: What's that?

SUBJECT: He said, "You know you are."

DAVID: Well, that's good, thank you, because I didn't know if there are other things we should add beyond golden divine light and all. I think the reincarnation things and meeting your council is important to find yourself, and realizing your divine nature.

Well, I want to thank the council. Thank you for the time and allowing her to go deep and learn more about herself and her past. And a lot of gratitude for sharing that time with us and I appreciate it.

SUBJECT: [Deep, sleepy breathing]

DAVID: And as we talk, -------------, we're going to gently raise up. To five we're going to count all the way up, from zero to five. On each higher number you're finding yourself more and more awake, feeling more and more awake. Feeling a sense of power inside and feeling all the pain gone in the stomach. Seeing that golden light in your mind and in your stomach. And feeling yourself waking up more and more, as we count up from one to two.

Waking up more and more, more and more. And as we count up to three on to four, you feel yourself becoming more awake, feeling so good inside. So relaxed. And as we count up to five, you're starting to blink your eyes and stretch. You're enjoying the feeling, but you feel like you want to wake up. You feel like you just had a great nap and you just caught a great sleep. You're feeling yourself waking up. Do you feel yourself waking up?

SUBJECT: Yes.

DAVID: How do you feel?

SUBJECT: I could hear you.

DAVID: What?

SUBJECT: I felt like I was asleep, but I could hear you, and I couldn't wake up.

DAVID: Like you could hear me from a distance or something?

SUBJECT: Yes.

DAVID: Like in a tunnel?

SUBJECT: Yes.

DAVID: So, you feel pretty good over all?

SUBJECT: I am.

DAVID: And how is your pain?

SUBJECT: It's not bothering me. I have no pain. That's really weird.

A Love that Couldn't Be

~

This reading was conducted with a female subject in her mid-thirties. The subject recounts another life she had that took place over 150 years ago. As we were to learn, it was with the same man who is her ex-husband in this life, referred to as Eric.

DAVID: [Hypnotic induction ends] Okay, feeling so relaxed. So relaxed. And in your mind's eye, I want you to picture another time, another place, when you were a different person, but you know it was you. Before the life as --------------- now, the life of the person before you became -----------. And I want you to visualize it in your mind, and you can tell me what you see.

SUBJECT: [Long pause] [Very softly] Eric… Eric was here.

DAVID: Say that again? What do you see?

SUBJECT: Eric.

DAVID: You see Eric? Is that what you said?

SUBJECT: Yes.

DAVID: And you see Eric, because, why?

SUBJECT: [Whispered] He's here. He's here at the house.

DAVID: He's at the house? And why did you see this house? Do you know why?

SUBJECT: No.

DAVID: You don't know why?

SUBJECT: He lives here.

DAVID: Okay, he lives there.

SUBJECT: He doesn't look… he looks different.

DAVID: He looks different now? But you know it's him?

SUBJECT: Mhm [yes].

DAVID: So, you're picturing a house. Do you live with Eric?

SUBJECT: No.

DAVID: No? But you think it's his house? How old does the house look?

SUBJECT: It's…

DAVID: Does it look very old?

SUBJECT: It doesn't have electricity.

DAVID: Say that again?

SUBJECT: It doesn't have power. There's no power.

DAVID: Oh, there's no power in the house. So, it's a pretty old house, then? It's pretty far back. Does it feel about the 1800s?

SUBJECT: Yes.

DAVID: Does it look kind of like a cabin?

SUBJECT: Kind of.

DAVID: Now that you know its Eric, what does he look like?

SUBJECT: He's tall.

DAVID: He's taller than he is now?

SUBJECT: He's very tall. Taller than he is now.

DAVID: Do you know what state you're in? Or where this house is located? Do you know where?

SUBJECT: No. In a desert.

DAVID: Say that again?

SUBJECT: It's like a desert.

DAVID: The desert? And why are you there? Do you live in the area too or where are you from?

SUBJECT: [Whispered] I don't know.

DAVID: Okay, but you see a house somewhere out in the desert? Do you see cactus and sand?

SUBJECT: It's bare.

DAVID: It's just bare?

SUBJECT: Mhm [yes].

DAVID: Now, do you know what Eric does for a living in that life?

SUBJECT: No.

DAVID: But you know yourself. What do you do for a living? Do you remember?

SUBJECT: [Softly] I don't know.

DAVID: You're not sure?

SUBJECT: There's children.

DAVID: You take care of children?

SUBJECT: There's children.

DAVID: You have children?

SUBJECT: Yes.

DAVID: How many children do you have?

SUBJECT: [Mumbled] Eight.

DAVID: How many?

SUBJECT: Eight.

DAVID: You have eight children? And they were all yours?

SUBJECT: Yes.

DAVID: What's your husband's name?

SUBJECT: I don't know. He's dead.

DAVID: But you have eight children. And do you see your husband in your mind? What does he look like?

SUBJECT: [Soft sounds like crying].

DAVID: And remember, we're just observing. So, don't get caught up in that life emotionally. Can you do that for me?

SUBJECT: Mhm [yes].

DAVID: So, what does your husband look like in this life?

SUBJECT: He has a beard.

DAVID: He has a beard. What color is his beard?

SUBJECT: Gray.

DAVID: A gray beard. And what do you look like?

SUBJECT: I'm short.

DAVID: You're short, and what color is your hair?

SUBJECT: Black.

DAVID: You have black hair. Do you consider yourself pretty, or do other people think you're pretty?

SUBJECT: Yes.

DAVID: But you don't look like you do now, is that correct?

SUBJECT: No, I don't.

DAVID: And you had eight children. Now what did your husband do for a living?

SUBJECT: Farmer.

DAVID: Did you grow a lot of different crops? Did you help some in the fields or did he have people help him?

SUBJECT: I didn't… I didn't like the cow.

DAVID: You didn't like the cow? Was he mean?

SUBJECT: I just didn't like it.

DAVID: You just didn't like the cow?

SUBJECT: Uh-uh [no].

DAVID: Do you remember the cow's name?

SUBJECT: Uh-uh [no].

DAVID: And why didn't you like the cow?

SUBJECT: I don't know.

DAVID: So, when you look around in your mind's eye, do you see the children running around?

SUBJECT: Mhm [yes].

DAVID: And give me some names of the children. Do you remember any of them?

SUBJECT: [Long pause] [Incomprehensible mumbling] Matthew.

DAVID: Okay, and who else?

SUBJECT: I don't know.

DAVID: Now as you're sitting there looking at all the children, I want you to go into the future with me. I want you to go farther into that life. Go ten years into the future in that life, and I want you to picture a big event that took place in your life, that you remember that meant something to you in that life. Do you see anything?

SUBJECT: No.

DAVID: How long did you live in that life? Do you remember?

SUBJECT: Not long. I died.

DAVID: You died? Say that again?

SUBJECT: I died.

DAVID: Okay, now let's just observe that life. I don't want you to get emotionally involved. Let's just observe it. Nice and relaxed. Just observing that life and death. Do you know what you died from?

SUBJECT: [Long pause]

DAVID: So, you don't know?

SUBJECT: [Incomprehensible mumble]

DAVID: What? What was it?

SUBJECT: Something my heart, my chest.

DAVID: Something with your heart?

SUBJECT: Yes.

DAVID: Do you think it was a heart attack?

SUBJECT: No.

DAVID: Something else?

SUBJECT: Somebody hurt me.

DAVID: Somebody what?

SUBJECT: Hurt me.

DAVID: Hurt you?

SUBJECT: Yes. [Quick, anxious breathing]

DAVID: Now don't get emotionally involved. We're just looking at the life. So, I want you to step back. I'm here with you. I'm here with you observing that life with you. So, you're safe. You have that bubble of protection around you too. Don't forget that. So, they hurt you, and it hurt your heart and killed you?

SUBJECT: Yes.

DAVID: Was it somebody you knew or was it a stranger?

SUBJECT: Somebody…

DAVID: Somebody what?

SUBJECT: Somebody I knew.

DAVID: Somebody you knew?

SUBJECT: It was Eric.

DAVID: So, you think it might have been Eric that did it?

SUBJECT: [Mumbled] It was his wife.

DAVID: And why would Eric do that? Did you ever know why?

SUBJECT: [Long pause]

DAVID: Do you know why he would do that?

SUBJECT: It was his wife.

DAVID: His what?

SUBJECT: His wife.

DAVID: Oh, his wife, told him to kill you?

SUBJECT: Yes.

DAVID: And why did she want you dead? Were you having an affair?

SUBJECT: No.

DAVID: So why would she want to kill you? Did she not like you?

SUBJECT: [Barely audible whisper] We loved each other.

DAVID: What?

SUBJECT: We loved each other.

DAVID: You loved each other?

SUBJECT: Yes.

DAVID: In that life?

SUBJECT: Yes.

DAVID: And what else can you tell me?

SUBJECT: It's different.

DAVID: Say that again?

SUBJECT: It's different.

DAVID: It was different? Even though you were both married, or you were before your husband died, you had a love at the time that was Eric, is that true?

SUBJECT: Yes.

DAVID: So, if Eric was in love, why did he kill you?

SUBJECT: [Mumbled] Love at first sight.

DAVID: What?

SUBJECT: Love at first sight.

DAVID: In that life?

SUBJECT: Yes.

DAVID: Well, here's what we want to do now. As we look at that life, how did he…?

SUBJECT: He stabbed me. [Quick, upset breathing]

DAVID: [With emphasis] Remember we're just observing. We're just observing. Now, right at the moment of death, as you see yourself — and we're just observing — I want you to tell me when you fell on the floor, right at the moment of death, did you see yourself standing outside of your body? What do you remember?

SUBJECT: [Mumbled] Looking at my body on the ground.

DAVID: You saw your body on the ground?

SUBJECT: Yes.

DAVID: And then how long did you stay there? Did somebody come to get you, to help you?

SUBJECT: Eric. He fell to the ground and cried.

DAVID: He cried? So, you watched him cry over your body?

SUBJECT: I wanted him not to cry.

DAVID: You didn't want him to cry?

SUBJECT: No.

DAVID: And you couldn't stop him though, could you?

SUBJECT: No.

DAVID: Because you knew at that moment…

SUBJECT: He didn't have a choice.

DAVID: You felt he didn't really have a choice, and you forgave him for taking your life while you're standing there, I guess, is that correct?

SUBJECT: I loved him.

DAVID: Because you loved him, right?

SUBJECT: Yes.

DAVID: Okay, now I want you to do this. I want you to look at that scene, but I want you to go somewhere else soon. How long did you stay?

SUBJECT: Hours.

DAVID: You stayed there hours?

SUBJECT: It felt like hours. I just want him to stop crying.

DAVID: Did he ever get caught for killing you?

SUBJECT: I don't know.

DAVID: You don't remember? Well, let me ask you this: After that happened and you're lying there, and you're watching him while you're standing outside of your body, watching him cry... You stayed in the scene for hours, I'm going to go past the hours that you stayed there, and I want you to tell me where you went after that. Where did your spirit go?

SUBJECT: Some place.

DAVID: Say that again?

SUBJECT: I don't know. Some place. I just went there.

DAVID: So, your soul went to some place you know. Was it heaven?

SUBJECT: It's not really.

DAVID: Well, what was it like when you got to the other side? What did it look like?

SUBJECT: Different.

DAVID: Different than here?

SUBJECT: Yes.

DAVID: Can you give me some background and describe it to me a little bit?

SUBJECT: [Mumbled] I'm not ready to be there.

DAVID: You what?

SUBJECT: I'm not ready to be there.

DAVID: You weren't ready to go to heaven, is that right?

SUBJECT: No, I'm not.

DAVID: Did you accept it? Or did it just feel like, "I want to go back to where I was instead"?

SUBJECT: I know it's where I belong.

DAVID: It's what?

SUBJECT: It's where I belong.

DAVID: Oh.

SUBJECT: I didn't want to be here yet.

DAVID: So, when you said you belonged, where is that place?

SUBJECT: It's where you go.

DAVID: Okay, was it dark or light?

SUBJECT: Bright.

DAVID: It was light?

SUBJECT: Yes.

DAVID: Did you see anybody else there that might have died before you? Was your mother or father there, or were they still alive?

SUBJECT: [Mumbled] There's chatter.

DAVID: What?

SUBJECT: There's chatter.

DAVID: There's chatter?

SUBJECT: Mhm [yes].

DAVID: Like a lot of voices going off at once?

SUBJECT: Mhm [yes].

DAVID: Does it seem pretty crowded?

SUBJECT: It's… [breathing] … too big. And there was room.

DAVID: So, there's plenty of room? Did you have…what kind of housing arrangements were there?

SUBJECT: It was crowded.

DAVID: It was what?

SUBJECT: Crowded.

DAVID: Now were you traumatized when you went to the other side? Did it take a while for you not to be upset?

SUBJECT: I didn't want to be there.

DAVID: You wanted to go back to where you were, is that correct?

SUBJECT: Yes.

DAVID: Did you miss your kids?

SUBJECT: [Long pause] Madelyn.

DAVID: Who's Madelyn?

SUBJECT: My daughter.

DAVID: Did you miss her too?

SUBJECT: [Quiet crying]

DAVID: Now we're just observing. Don't get emotionally caught up in it. We're just observing.

SUBJECT: Yes.

DAVID: What was your name?

SUBJECT: I don't know.

DAVID: You don't remember. But you know you had a daughter named Madelyn, right?

SUBJECT: Margot. Silas.

DAVID: Margot? Margot Silas?

SUBJECT: Silas.

DAVID: Silas? Like, S-I-L-A-S?

SUBJECT: Yes.

DAVID: And what was your husband's first name?

SUBJECT: Silas.

DAVID: Oh, that was his name?

SUBJECT: Yes.

DAVID: Do you remember your last name?

SUBJECT: No.

DAVID: Okay, so it was Margot and Silas. And you said you had eight children, is that correct?

SUBJECT: Yes.

DAVID: And he was a farmer and you were a housewife and kept the place up, I guess?

SUBJECT: Taught the children.

DAVID: Okay, taught the children.

SUBJECT: I taught them…how to keep the farm.

DAVID: Say that again?

SUBJECT: I taught them how to keep up the farm.

DAVID: Did you have a well?

SUBJECT: Yes.

DAVID: And what did you grow on that farm? Do you remember?

SUBJECT: Corn.

DAVID: Mostly corn?

SUBJECT: And cabbage. There's buffalo. They're not…

DAVID: There's buffalo?

SUBJECT: There's buffalo.

DAVID: That must have been neat to see. Were they fun to watch?

SUBJECT: [Whispered] They're big.

DAVID: Big herds of them?

SUBJECT: Yes.

DAVID: Now what state do you think you were living in?

SUBJECT: I don't know.

DAVID: You don't remember? Let me ask you this. That's a very interesting life though tragic. And as we go forward, let me ask a few more questions. When you went back to heaven, where you went after death, I want you to sit there and look around. You said you can hear chatter. Who came and met you when you got there, do you remember?

SUBJECT: Yes.

DAVID: And who was it?

SUBJECT: The greeter.

DAVID: The greeter. Were they one of your spirit guides or how did you know them?

SUBJECT: No.

DAVID: Oh, you don't know?

SUBJECT: No, they're taking me.

DAVID: They're taking you?

SUBJECT: Yes.

DAVID: And where are they taking you to?

SUBJECT: To talk.

DAVID: To what?

SUBJECT: To talk about that life.

DAVID: So, they want to talk to you about that life you had? [Pause, waiting for response] Is that correct?

SUBJECT: [Whispered] Yes.

DAVID: Were they nice and loving?

SUBJECT: Yes.

DAVID: Was it a council talking about your life?

SUBJECT: Yes.

DAVID: As you're sitting in the council room talking to your council, what color is your soul? What colors do you give off?

SUBJECT: Teal.

DAVID: Or greenish blue, I guess, right?

SUBJECT: It's green with blue.

DAVID: Green and blue. So, it's a pretty color, isn't it?

SUBJECT: Yes.

DAVID: That's neat. And what are some of the council member's colors? What colors are their souls?

SUBJECT: Purple.

DAVID: Purple? Any gold or just all purple?

SUBJECT: Yes, there's gold.

DAVID: There was some gold in there too?

SUBJECT: Yes.

DAVID: Do you see Jesus or anyone there?

SUBJECT: No.

DAVID: Do you see any archangels?

SUBJECT: No.

DAVID: Okay, but you see your council, and a lot of them have purple souls. Is that correct?

SUBJECT: Yes. They're talking about me but not to me.

DAVID: Say that again?

SUBJECT: They're talking about me but not to me.

DAVID: Oh, they're talking about you. Can you hear them in your mind telepathically?

SUBJECT: No, I'm observing.

DAVID: Oh, you're observing. Did they have anything resembling holographic screens to show you of your life?

SUBJECT: No.

DAVID: But you know they're talking, correct?

SUBJECT: Yes.

DAVID: And they're going over the life you just had as Margot?

SUBJECT: Yes.

DAVID: What do they think of that life? Did they have any issues with part of that life? What would you say to that?

SUBJECT: [Long pause] Yes.

DAVID: Tell me about it.

SUBJECT: [Pause] I don't know.

DAVID: Okay, they weren't mad or upset by you having an affair with Eric?

SUBJECT: I didn't have an affair.

DAVID: Oh, you didn't?

SUBJECT: I just loved him.

DAVID: So, you loved him, and he loved you, but you never had an affair?

SUBJECT: No.

DAVID: So, you saw each other and that was it? Love at first sight but you guys never kissed or anything?

SUBJECT: Never.

DAVID: Never? How did the wife know about you then?

SUBJECT: Because [pause] they stayed with us.

DAVID: Say that again?

SUBJECT: They stayed on our farm.

DAVID: Oh, so Eric and his wife stayed on your farm too, right?

SUBJECT: Yes.

DAVID: But the wife thought you were having an affair. Is that correct?

SUBJECT: No.

DAVID: She did not feel you were having an affair, but she still wanted him to kill you?

SUBJECT: [Sounds of crying]

DAVID: You're just observing, don't get caught up in it. We're just observing the life together. But you feel… what did you learn in that life that meant a lot to you? What did you learn? Was there anything in particular?

SUBJECT: Patience.

DAVID: Say that again?

SUBJECT: Patience.

DAVID: Patience. You learned patience in that life? Good. Any other lessons that you learned?

SUBJECT: Patience with my daughter.

DAVID: Patience with your daughter?

SUBJECT: Patience with my daughter, Madelyn.

DAVID: Okay. Well, it was a quick and tragic life. You saw some cool buffalo. You had a lot of children. Do you see your own funeral?

SUBJECT: No.

DAVID: Can't see it? Let's try counting down a little bit. Feeling so relaxed. And as we count down, I want you to remember as you leave that life, just leaving that life behind. And as we count down, I want you to see if there are other things you can tell me. As you leave that life and you're now back in your bubble, feeling so relaxed. And I want you to look in your mind's eye. Do you feel any angels around you on the other side?

SUBJECT: Yes.

DAVID: Okay, and what angels come to you? Do you know their names?

SUBJECT: [very softly] Philomena.

DAVID: Helelina?

SUBJECT: Philomena.

DAVID: Oh, Philomena, okay. Does she help you?

SUBJECT: Yes.

DAVID: Does she protect you and talk to you?

SUBJECT: She's my greeter.

DAVID: She's your greeter?

SUBJECT: Yes.

DAVID: What color is her soul? What kind of light does she put off?

SUBJECT: [Whispered] Purple.

DAVID: She's purple too. Is she a pretty purple?

SUBJECT: [Barely audible] Yes.

DAVID: Does she have a lot of energy?

SUBJECT: [Barely audible] Yes.

DAVID: Do you feel safer when you're around her?

SUBJECT: [Barely audible] Yes.

DAVID: Could she come in the room with us now while we're here? Could you ask her to come here?

SUBJECT: No.

DAVID: So, you don't think she'll come talk to us?

SUBJECT: No.

DAVID: Okay, but that's your greeter that greeted you, right?

[In many regressions, it is not always possible to have a subject's spirit guides or council offer advice for the subject concerning the life they are currently living. Though they realize I'm trying to help the subject move forward in their life, there are times when they feel certain information should not be shared or the subject is not yet ready to receive. I decided to try harder to see if we could get her greeter to help the subject with things she needed to work on in this life.]

SUBJECT: Yes.

DAVID: And you have dealt with her in other lives too, I bet? She's been with you a long time?

SUBJECT: Yes.

DAVID: So, she knows you pretty well, doesn't she?

SUBJECT: Yes.

DAVID: Okay. So, if we talk to Philomena, can we ... well, that's nice that you have such a beautiful greeter, that's special.

SUBJECT: [Breathing as though asleep]

DAVID: What does Philomena say about this life you're in as ------------ now?

SUBJECT: [Breathing as though asleep]

DAVID: What does Philomena think ------------ should be working on? What part of the soul contract that you signed should you work on? What are some things you need to learn in this life?

SUBJECT: Perseverance.

DAVID: Say that again?

SUBJECT: Perseverance.

DAVID: Perseverance. So, you're working on that in this life, is that right?

SUBJECT: Yes.

DAVID: Is there anything else in this life you're working on?

SUBJECT: [Breathing deeply as though asleep]

DAVID: No? But, definitely perseverance, right?

SUBJECT: Yes. Staying true.

DAVID: Okay, staying true. And what else?

SUBJECT: [Breathing deeply]

DAVID: Those are good lessons. Are there any other ones?

SUBJECT: [Breathing deeply]

DAVID: Well, I think we covered a lot of ground today, don't you? So, as we leave this session, I want you to stay relaxed and remember in your mind the things you've learned that you need to work on. You're feeling more relaxed. You're feeling your heart rate slow down. And you're feeling yourself coming back as we count from zero up to five.

[Before the session, the client had mentioned she felt very anxious and stressed. She shared that her monitoring bracelet had showed her heart rate over 127 beats per minute on average over the previous several hours. Her normal rate was around 55-60 beats per minute.]

You're going to feel yourself becoming more and more awake. Feeling you are coming back. Feeling yourself waking up. Feeling your heart rate steady to its normal rhythm. Allowing yourself to wake up. As we count from one to two. Feeling yourself coming up more and more, coming back. Feeling you are coming back to today. As we count from two to three, you're feeling yourself coming more awake. But still feeling so relaxed, feeling so much better inside. Feeling all this love and happiness in your heart. Feeling all the stress gone and feeling your confidence go higher and higher as I count from three to four. Feeling so good, so relaxed.

Now you'll be able to sleep tonight. All those things that occupy your mind and make you anxious and stressed, going forward, you will put them outside of you. You will keep them outside of you and shut the doors you create in your mind and lock it. Don't take them to bed with you so when you wake up you don't think about them. You just leave them away from you behind locked doors. When you have to deal with them, you open the doors and deal with them, then afterward put them back behind the closed doors and lock it. That's where you're going to keep those, not inside you anymore. You're going to keep those at a distance, locked away, and outside of you. This will bring your stress and anxiety down immensely. It will also help you with your stomach issues caused by this turmoil your experiencing in your personal life.

You feel yourself waking up more, starting to stretch out a little bit. Feeling so relaxed. As we count from four to five. Stretching more and more, growing more and more awake.

[Subject awake and stretching]

SUBJECT: [glancing at monitoring bracelet] That's amazing.

DAVID: What is?

SUBJECT: [showing me bracelet] My heart rate was fifty-seven during the session and still is!

DAVID: Good stuff. Listen to this recording and take Philomena's advice to heart and lock those worries outside of you. Should help to keep your blood pressure, heart rate and anxiety down.

The Universal Laws

~

"The Principles of the Truth are Seven; he who knows these, understandingly, possesses the Magic Key whose touch will fly open all the Doors of the Temple—the Universe exists by virtue of these Laws, which form its framework, and which hold it together."

—The Seven Great Hermetic Principles

The Seven Universal Laws or Principles by which everything in the Universe is governed have excellent application to our individual lives. It is hard for anyone to imagine that our personal lives are so impacted by these Universal Laws, yet everything we think, our actions, our deeds, our desires, exist in perfect harmony with these laws. These laws are ancient, and it is difficult to pinpoint any one single source where they originated. There are whispers of these laws in every religion, from the Bible, Koran, Vedic texts, Buddhism, Confucianism, to ancient writings and secret teachings dating back thousands of years. Every one of them has at its core these spiritual and ancient truths, and ascended masters, sages, and prophets of the past have shared these with many.

Learning these laws, understanding their significance, and applying them well in your life will bring about positive benefits and transform your life in ways you never thought possible. Three of the Universal Laws are immutable, eternal Laws. They can never be changed and will never change. It is impossible to alter them, and they transcend all there is and go back to the beginning of everything. Nothing can affect them, and they are absolute. The last four laws can be altered and can be manipulated. This means with good effort and study, you can bend them to your will and accomplish things you may never have thought possible.

Whether you learn to apply or use these laws correctly in your life, these seven laws will still govern your entire existence. By understanding and mastering these Seven Universal laws, you will find yourself in the driver's seat in your personal life, relationships, business dealings, and with whomever you interact in all facets of your life.

1. The Law of Mentalism

The immutable Law of Mentalism states that everything we know as reality in our physical world has its origin in the unseen or spiritual realms. It refers to the Collective Consciousness, GOD, Spirit, Source, Brahma, Yahweh, or whatever name you associate with the Universal Mind in your beliefs or religious structure. This Universal Mind permeates from the lowest dimensions to the highest. All life, whether of the animal, mineral, or plant kingdom has its origins in this law. All things manifest from this law, and it cannot be changed or altered. Everything in all universes is subject to this law from energy, matter, dark matter, gravity and everything not yet discovered by science. Everyone on this planet and all life throughout the cosmos is part of the Universal Mind. The reality all of us create is a manifestation of our mind, and our mind is a piece of the Universal Mind.

2. The Law of Correspondence

The second of the immutable laws is the Law of Correspondence. The phrase many are familiar with comes from this immutable law and tells us, "As above, so below; as below, so above." Agreement and correspondence exist on all realms. Whether on the physical planes, in the mental realms, or on any of the spiritual dimensions, everything is connected, everything is in agreement, and there is correspondence with everything.

This immutable law means everything is connected throughout the Universe, including everyone on this planet and everything else throughout the universe(s). Everything originates from the same One Source. It does not matter whether we are referring to the smallest atom or electron or the most massive star or planet, everything is ONE, and this pattern is expressed throughout the Universe.

3. The Law of Vibration

The last immutable law is the Law of Vibration. Everything in the universe is pure energy, and this includes the physical, spiritual and mental planes. Even what we consider "solid," like our bodies, pets, buildings, rocks, plants, moons, and planets, are just vibrating energy. Everything vibrates, and it is only a matter of degree or frequency how much motion or vibration an object or condition exhibits. For example, denser materials or objects exposed to frigid temperatures tend to vibrate less on average. Conversely, objects in a highly excitable state, exposed to high temperature, in vapor form, or in higher dimensional states, tend to vibrate more. Science today has confirmed what the ancients, ascended masters, philosophers like Plato, Socrates, Aristotle, and in certain ancient texts like the Vedic, among other sources, have known for eons: *Everything is always moving.*

The "Law of Attraction" — similar energies attract similar energy — has its foundation in this Law. We experience life through our five senses, and since all senses vibrate, they are transferred instantaneously to our brain. Once entering our brain as vibrating energy, we will react in infinite ways depending on how we process the information we are receiving. For example, if we act negatively or feel negative, sad or depressed in our thoughts, we can potentially attract other energies that are exhibiting similar reactions to the varied stimuli. If we approach adverse events that befall us, disappointments that we experience in life — whether in our career, relationships or health — in a dark fashion, we can make them even worse.

The lightest vibration that exists is unconditional love for another, while hate, ego, greed, and fear are among the densest. The student who learns to control their thoughts, actions, and deeds throughout life will find themselves attracting positive energies, having more success in life, and finding greater fulfillment and joy. Those that cannot control their negative thoughts or actions will often find themselves leading a life dogged by disappointments, struggle and consumed by darkness. Basking in the incredible possibilities of what living in the light represents, by having good thoughts, followed by deeds and actions geared toward the benefit of all, will find you experiencing rewarding outcomes throughout your life.

4. The Law of Polarity

The Law of Polarity is the first of the mutable laws, which states that there are two sides to everything and what appears as opposite is only a matter of degree. Meaning everything we think, whether something is hot or cold for example, is the polar opposite of the other at extremes. Everything is paired, opposites are identical, and everything has poles, and the only difference is by degree. Love and hate, light or dark, good and evil, peace or war, are a matter of degree. Learning to transform your thoughts by raising your vibrations consciously can change your life toward one of happiness, greater abundance, and satisfaction in your interactions. In the ancient Hermetic Teachings, learning how to manipulate the Law of Polarity by always focusing on the "best intents" in your interactions with others will find you rising above this law in ways to your benefit.

Remember everything is connected, everything is ONE and GOD, or Spirit is above opposites. Always strive for the good in situations even when things are going badly. In doing this you will see the pendulum move back in a positive direction sooner than if you had stayed negative and focused on the darkness of the situation. Strive for that.

5. The Law of Rhythm

The Law of Rhythm is the second of the mutable laws. It lets us know that everything rises or falls, whether nations, stock markets, tides, or anything else you can think of. This Law of Rhythm operates like a pendulum, swinging from one side to the other and manifests itself in everything. Our thoughts are significantly affected by this law and all of us have seen our reactions turn from positive to negative depending on the external event or stimuli. How well you can control your reactions and how successfully you can cope with negativity in your life, relationships or career determines the swing. The more significant your control in how you view things in life, the more the pendulum will move in a positive direction for you. Your success or failure in life, what you pursue, and your interactions with others are significantly affected by this law and a major determinant of how happy you are in general.

To become a master of this law requires strengthening your ability to be aware of the backward movement in anything you undertake or pursue. Noticing the subtle shift of anything you set in motion — whether involving your relationships, career, health, or any goal you may have — allows you a greater ability to reverse the movement. Whenever you notice the Law start to draw you away from your desires, vision or aims, do not lose hope, but try to go forward with determination and keep your eye on the prize you are seeking.

Remain focused on your outcome and what you're looking to accomplish and work diligently to remain positive even when it seems too difficult to maintain, no matter how long it takes. If your efforts meet with failure, find comfort that by having patience and staying positive, eventually the motion will reverse and move back in the direction you prefer.

Work hard to understand how these Laws work and how to apply them, and you will notice significant improvements in your life. Over time, your dedication will be rewarded as the backward movements will become less severe, and the pendulum of your life hovers more in the positive direction you always wanted.

6. The Law of Cause and Effect

Few in life apply this third mutable law correctly. They often find themselves hostage to their thoughts, and these thoughts are often intimately connected to one's actions. Everything we set in motion is governed by the Law of Cause and Effect: Every cause has its effect, and every effect has its cause. Everything that takes place that you affect and manifest in your outside or physical world has a definite origin in your mind and consciousness. This means every one of your thoughts, deeds or actions has significance and will set a specific event in motion. The effects that you set in motion will eventually materialize over time. By controlling your thoughts for the betterment of not only yourself, but all you encounter, will find you a master of your destiny and reward you in ways you may have thought impossible early on. Controlling your thoughts and actions will find you consumed with good things in your life.

Creative imagery, focused meditation, visualization, and applying proper intentions, or specifically, "Good Cause" will lead to outcomes that serve your highest good and what you create in the physical world. Your thoughts are powerful and affect all the outcomes in your life, positively or negatively. This law ultimately affects every plane of existence, whether on the physical, mental or spiritual plane. Learn to use this law effectively, pay attention to your thoughts and guard your actions carefully. You will be amazed at what good things may come your way.

7. The Law of Gender

The last of the mutable laws, the Law of Gender, states that everything has its masculine and feminine qualities. This law has its roots in all of creation, whether plants, minerals, humans or animals. Everything contains both masculine and feminine qualities.

We all know men who are nicer than others, more compassionate and loving. These traits are typically considered more feminine than masculine. Among women friends, we all have known someone at one time or another who was more athletic, competitive, and the leader or captain of any sports teams they were involved with. These are typically considered more masculine attributes.

Most define feminine attributes as being nurturing, more loving, caring, compassionate and patient than their male counterparts. Most identify masculine traits as greater self-reliance, hunting, leading, and protecting, which are more prevalent among men. All of us possess both masculine and feminine qualities, and it is only a matter of degree which traits are more prevalent.

To master this Law, one must accept that everything exhibits both feminine and masculine qualities. Lying within every woman exist masculine traits and within every man are feminine attributes. Mastering this Law requires one to be balanced. In other words, one needs equal amounts of love, compassion, patience, and intuition, offset by the masculine attributes of self-reliance, leadership, energy, and logic. One who finds balance with this law will have better interactions with both sexes and more fulfilling and successful relationships in all areas of their life.

Conclusion

~

"The journey to enlightenment is not easy; it requires great patience, an unquenchable thirst for knowledge, truth, and understanding, as well as a strong belief in one's self. The way is within, for only by going inside can one discover their true self and the divinity of all."

Every step we take in the direction of knowing ourselves takes us closer to the realization of our infinite nature and unbounded possibilities as Divine souls. We can take these steps through learning of our past lives, our life between lives, research, growing through experiences, and by sharing and exchanging knowledge with others. Most importantly, each step brings us closer to enlightenment.

Though our progress may seem slow at times, maintaining patience and learning to apply the Seven Universal Laws correctly in our lives will find us moving toward a greater understanding of reality and a future we want.

In many cases, the lives shared by the subjects in these case studies were quite challenging and difficult. The majority of the subjects taken through regression were evolved souls based on the material they shared while in a hypnotic state and my personal experience conducting readings.

I have found that those with many incarnations and experiences often take quite demanding lives to accelerate their soul growth and evolvement. The lives, lessons and bodies they choose when incarnating, and who they interact with to help them with their chosen life lessons, are carefully considered in advance with their spirit guides and councils. While "life" to some reading this book may seem like an unending boot camp fraught with perils and difficulty, remember our free will enables us to have a lot of leeway in the choices we make and lessons we take when incarnating to help us advance in the spirit world.

By accepting challenging lives and passing the lessons we chose for an incarnation, our soul strengthens in the process. Even when subjected to what seems a tragic or unforgiving set of circumstances within a particularly difficult life, how we respond and stand-up to trials and tribulations will determine how well we did with that series of events upon review by our Council.

While some may approach the role of a Council as judgmental and demanding, nothing is farther from the truth. Our Councils are there to guide us and help us with only our best intents in mind. It's no different than how loving and wise parents are to a child, helping them grow to adulthood with experienced advice and lessons. They are benevolent mentors, evolved beings who have had many experiences in their numerous incarnations and are well suited to help us make the best decisions for our highest interests.

Growing in awareness helps to light our way and when faced with difficult forks on our journey through life, pausing and drawing upon our intuition, knowledge, and previous experiences will aid us in making the best choices for our life possibilities. More often than not, by reflecting on what we're considering, adding prayer and meditation, and creating a well-thought-out plan, we will find ourselves more times than not on a route that is in our best interest and will lead us to the best outcomes for our soul growth.

Being cognizant of the interconnectivity of everything at all levels — whether involving other human beings, animals, planets, galaxies, and universes — sets us up for greater understanding of infinite possibility. When faced with adversity, we are the beneficiaries, because it is how we learn to stand up to failure and setbacks, which marks our progress in life and helps us to evolve.

Sometimes, the lessons we accept in our lives seem too painful to get through or beyond. Our mind, when faced with daunting tasks, can often turn negative, leaving us with a weakened ability to accept what has befallen us, making the life lessons we have chosen that much more challenging to complete.

If we learn to approach difficult circumstances or challenges in our lives as just another test and try to bend the mutable Universal

Laws to our advantage, we can turn even what seems the most negative situation to a positive experience. By just giving ourselves the benefit of the doubt when times are tough, holding great patience, and believing in ourselves, often we can turn the most trying of times into something brighter.

The greatest thing we can learn on our soul journey is to try and let go of a difficult past, adapt and find success out of what we perceive as the ashes of our former self. Rising again like the Phoenix and working to create a new and enjoyable life for ourselves, will often find us able to make something out of what we thought was lost.

Often what we mistake as missing or incomplete in our lives is the failure to recognize we have the power to reverse our course by applying the Universal Laws correctly. Enlightenment, at its core, is finding ourselves. Growth in wisdom comes with time and crowns those who seek eternal knowledge and understanding.

I hope this book helps you on your journey and that the path you are on in this life takes you to fulfilled dreams and completed lessons. When death beckons once more may it bring the promise of a heartfelt and joyful reunion with your guides, soul group, departed loved ones, and council after crossing over and joining them again in the higher realms.

Acknowledgements

I'd be remiss if I didn't reach deep into my childhood and acknowledge the fellow Boy Scout who intrigued other scouts and me with his amateur, but effective hypnotic induction on a fellow scout. That demonstration stuck in my mind and helped to plant the first seed on my journey of self-discovery. To my guides, who probably had some hand in my very random flipping through channels on a rare day off work and stopping on a channel demonstrating past life regressions, which nudged me to try my first regression. To the hypnotist who opened doors for me in my subconscious enabling me to learn more of myself. Watching her maneuver three audience participants into a hypnotic state, where they recounted markedly different lives from their current one, intrigued and motivated me to continue on my path of self-discovery. By pulling back the veil into my past, she allowed me several glimpses of who I AM and what existed in the spirit world. Thank you and to you, I am very grateful.

To the ascended masters who have come before, such as Jesus, Buddha, Confucius, Rama, Mohammed, and the wisdom they have shared on how to live, love and be. To other great thinkers like Plato, Socrates, Newton, Da Vinci, Einstein, among others, thank you for your contributions to mankind. To those incredible explorers who have delved into the conscious, subconscious and super-conscious aspects of our mind in more recent times, who have aided myself and others through their works: Dr. Carl Jung, Dr. Michael Newton, Edgar Cayce, Dr. Byron Weiss, Robert Monroe, among many more, I give great thanks. Every one of you has been instrumental in progressing my journey, not only to find myself, but in helping to open many doors to the spiritual and mental realms. To Natalie, her assistance in editing, editorial suggestions, cover design, and overall support during the process, made this a better book than it would have been otherwise. To my dear readers, thank you for taking this journey with me and hopefully sharing what you have learned to help others on their journey through life and beyond.

Best Regards,

David

~

About the Author

~

David Rippy attended Villanova University before graduating from Texas A&M University with a Bachelor of Science degree in Economics. At age twenty-five, he was just beginning a career at a Fortune 50 company when a car accident left him paralyzed from the shoulders down.

Despite this life-altering injury, he formulated a vision for his life. He became determined to fulfill his ambition to become a money manager—and he did. David went on to have a long and successful career. He worked at Merrill Lynch and the Vanguard Group for years and acquired various certifications and licenses in the process.

Today, he's left the finance field to write, speak, inspire and help others through hypnosis, healings, counseling, and sharing the story of his own perseverance and triumph. He is also the author of "Captain of my Soul: Mastering a Destiny Altered," and "Powering through Paralysis: How to Survive & Thrive with Disability or Disease." His website is visionpeakresources.com. He still believes that there are more miracles to come in his life and works toward new goals and aspirations every day.

Made in the
USA
Middletown, DE

76097765R00250